PRISON INDUSTRIAL COMPLEX
FOR BEGINNERS®

Praise for
Prison Industrial Complex For Beginners

"A truly indispensable book, especially for educators across the disciplines. One cannot understand America today without understanding the monstrosity that is the Prison Industrial Complex, and this slim volume helps readers not simply understand the PIC but feel righteous rage about it."

—BAZ DREISINGER
Associate Professor of English,
John Jay College of Criminal Justice;
Founding Academic Director,
Prison-to-College Pipeline;
author, *Incarceration Nations* (2016)

"In his penetrating *Prison Industrial Complex For Beginners,* Dr. Peterson shines a bright and relentless spotlight on the social catastrophe that is America's sprawling criminal justice system. As only an educator with a deep and personal knowledge of their subject material can, Peterson topples the myths and reveals the racist machinery that lies at the heart of that system. For too long, liberals and conservatives alike have labored under the delusion that the Prison Industrial Complex—when they even acknowledge its existence—is merely an unfortunate accident of history. It's as if it were a sort of natural disaster that, despite our best intentions, we've wandered aimlessly into. In clear and persuasive writing, Dr. Peterson argues that the human-ravaging machinery of the carceral state is the result of deliberate and racist policy, developed and strengthened at every level of government. *Prison Industrial Complex For Beginners* is essential reading for anyone curious about the origins of the harrowing path we've walked and hungry for the sort of clarity needed to lead the way out."

—GLENN E. MARTIN
JustLeadershipUSA

"Dr. James Braxton Peterson's *Prison Industrial Complex For Beginners* seamlessly patches together the complex development of the PIC, which is an overwhelming social and political force with many complicated causes and contributors. As a roadmap for understanding the United States' path to becoming known as Incarceration Nation, the book tracks why and how the US chose the road for implementing increasingly harsh punitive responses to crime instead of the route of embracing social solutions to address crime. Peterson's analysis illustrates how racism drove the choice to create and sustain a PIC that uses prisons for punishment and oppression as opposed to rehabilitation or social justice. By identifying policies related to the war on drugs, solitary confinement, life sentences for juveniles, exploitative inmate labor, prison privatization, as well as political verbiage that refers to prisoners as animals, Peterson's work highlights the dehumanization of people who are incarcerated as a central theme of American correctional policy."

—CAITLIN J. TAYLOR
Assistant Professor, Department of
Sociology and Criminal Justice
La Salle University

"In a highly engaging and straightforward manner, James Peterson locates, narrates, and critiques the massive apparatus that is today's American carceral state—one that has contained more black bodies, and has ensnared more black lives, than at any other point in U.S. history. For scholars and lay readers alike, Peterson's book makes clear that our nation's staggering rate of incarceration is not rooted in a disinterested policy response to violence or crime, nor has it become just some "rite of passage" for black youth. In short, mass incarceration's origins are deeply rooted in our nation's racialized past and, as importantly, it is today but one part of a massive Prison Industrial Complex that serves very specific interests, devastates communities, and therefore must be dismantled."

—HEATHER ANN THOMPSON
Historian, University of Michigan, and
author, *Blood in the Water:
The Attica Uprising of 1971 and its Legacy*
(2016)

PRISON INDUSTRIAL COMPLEX
FOR BEGINNERS®

BY
JAMES BRAXTON PETERSON

ILLUSTRATED BY
JOHN JENNINGS AND STACEY ROBINSON

FOREWORD BY
MICHAEL ERIC DYSON

FOR BEGINNERS®

For Beginners LLC
155 Main Street, Suite 211
Danbury, CT 06810 USA
www.forbeginnersbooks.com

A For Beginners® Documentary Comic Book
Copyright © 2016

Cataloging-in-Publication information is available from the Library of Congress.

ISBN-13 # 978-1-939994-31-8 Trade

Manufactured in the United States of America

For Beginners® and Beginners Documentary Comic Books® are published
by For Beginners LLC.

First Edition

10 9 8 7 6 5 4 3 2 1

Contents

Foreword

by Michael Eric Dyson

As a professor of English, James Braxton Peterson knows a thing or two about long, and wrong, sentences. Beyond his brilliant understanding of figures of speech, Peterson knows a great deal about the figures that simply don't add up to justice in the startling statistics of who gets locked up in modern America. And he knows about the human figures—black, brown, and poor—who end up in prison because of their color and not just their character.

I have occasionally accompanied Peterson as he burrows beneath the dingy confinement of "dangerous" human flesh inside jails and prisons. He has often conducted what can only be called an ethnography of imprisonment by asking the incarcerated what they think and feel. I have seen him ask about their mental and physical health, and about their families, before he rages, quietly and with great intelligence, against the forces that got them incarcerated. In terms at once poetic and practical, he translates Michel Foucault's reflections on discipline and punishment, or rap legend Nas's epistle to an imprisoned comrade caught up in the brutal logic of the streets, while never failing to think with them about the choices they made—choices that, in part, made them.

Because I am a clergyman, I viewed what Peterson was doing as ministry, indeed the most sophisticated and substantive ministry one might imagine without the proselytizing that is often seen as an evangelist's most compelling mission. Of course it is more than a little ironic that Peterson hails professionally from Pennsylvania, where a couple of centuries back the Quakers urged offenders to search their consciences in solitary confinement to piece back together their criminally fractured lives—a fateful trend that Peterson skillfully deconstructs in this book.

Peterson's mission in prison was different. He offered the victims of societal structures and behaviors an edifying twist on their destinies by urging them to become more conscious of what was being done to them, and what they were doing to themselves, in a society that cared little about the distinction and punished them all the same. Except it didn't punish them *all* the same. The matters of color and class and age and gender have to be figured in to recognize just how unjust our criminal justice system often is. Peterson not only embraced the ethnography of imprisonment in the situations he encountered, but he offered an on-the-spot, grassroots phenomenology of incarceration—a brief burst of empirical engagement with the entangled forces and dynamics that got folk imprisoned in the first place.

Consider *Prison Industrial Complex For Beginners* the remixed, extended version of Peterson's daring and compelling prison interventions. To be sure, the "industrial" in the title is more formal than substantial, except as a mark of the evolving understanding of a phenomenon with roots in the industrial era but that extends forward into the hyper-technological present. The means of surveillance and security that are part of the amped-up prison environment of today might suggest a shift in terminology to Prison Digital Complex, but then we'd lose the allusion to President Dwight Eisenhower's "Military-Industrial Complex" and every other variant of the term that seeks to link an area of government responsibility and private industry. In Eisenhower's case, it was the informal connection between the U.S. military and the defense industry; in the present case, it's the unseemly alliance between the nation's criminal justice system and the prison and punishment industry. Peterson, like social theorist Mike Davis who invented the term, has chosen to "PIC" this fight, and he's done it well. Those of us who read his book for beginners are the better for it.

It's all here, too: the things you need to know in order to understand how a behemoth and out-of-control system has taken root and colored our perception of criminal justice, how it has driven the need to reform the reformers—the John Wayne-infused Western frontier mythology that fuels the right-wing ideology of law-and-order, in which the ostensible protectors and servants of the law instead serve disorder and fuel injustice. Here is the chaotic and disastrous War on Drugs, too often a proxy war against people of color. Here, in stark reality and detail, is the privatization of prisons and the enormous, often immoral, profits that flow from vulnerable bodies locked away—bodies that are too often young, colored, female, and "foreign." For indeed the nation's immigration policies and the dreadful concomitant of solitary confinement have extended the international reach of our belligerently bloated PIC. And here is the suspect logic that drives both the paranoia about recidivism—which the legendary black preacher William Augustus Jones, Jr. defined as "a return in degree to a former state of being" (alluding in my view to the return of America to a racist past when it benefitted from unpaid black labor and the imprisonment that coerced it)—and the flawed ideals of prison reform that don't address the structural features of racial, gender, and class oppression.

This book is a sublimely useful powder keg—an explosive gathering of insight, information and, yes, inspiration, for us to act on what Peterson has learned and what he so valiantly teaches us. The ideas discussed here can't be restricted to those whose lives the PIC immediately impacts. Neither can they be confined to the souls whose existence is transformed by a loved one being locked away in hopeless dungeons of often unjust punishment. The bitter truth is that prisons affect all of us. We are all, to a degree, imprisoned by our thirst for the exclusion from society of its most vicious members. But the idea that prisons in America contain only the bodies of the righteously confined has been demolished by the volume of data rushing toward us from study after study, from book after book. Such work proves that our unstated class and color vengeance, and the rot of our gender bias, has spoiled our system of discipline and punishment—from the principal's office where kids of color are often unfair-

ly expelled, to jails where youth of color are often undeservedly detained, to prisons where adults of color are often unjustly confined. This book is Peterson's beautiful argument against an ugly reality.

Peterson and I often talk about the difficulties of doing work inside prisons and even just visiting them; my brother Everett has been incarcerated for nearly 30 years. But we never mistake our grief at being searched or the feeling of doom at doors being locked behind us as anything remotely approaching the dread and horror that those who are imprisoned must face every day. We simply pledge to never let those on the outside forget what those on the inside see and do, what they feel and think, what they experience and endure, and what we must do to bring an end to this grave injustice. James Braxton Peterson has kept his end of the bargain with this searing, insightful, and humane missive from a region where his brain and heart intersect. He sets his mind free to imagine what, hopefully one day soon, all people who are unjustly imprisoned, and even those who deserve a measure of punishment, can experience too.

Named by Ebony *magazine as one of the 100 most influential black Americans,* **Michael Eric Dyson** *is a renowned public intellectual, media commentator, and best-selling author whose most recent book is* The Black Presidency: Barack Obama and the Politics of Race in America *(2016). The University Professor of Sociology at Georgetown University, Dyson appears regularly on television as an analyst of political, racial, and cultural issues in America today. He is also an ordained Baptist minister and the former host of* The Michael Eric Dyson Show on *National Public Radio.*

Introduction

Growing up in Newark, New Jersey, in the 1980s, the specter of the Prison Industrial Complex was omnipresent. Even if I was not always consciously aware of the haunting impact that modern prison systems were making in my specific neighborhood, the consequences of the War on Drugs were both tangible and recognizable in my community. The constant police presence, the unstoppable erosion of residential life, and the unchecked violence of an underground economy were uninterrupted features of my youth in inner-city America.

As a pre-teen and later as a teenager, I never connected the dots of policies like the War on Drugs, or the economic shifts toward post-industrialism, to the disappearance of neighbors, friends, and family into an aggressive criminal justice system. Like many residents of Newark, I believed that better or more law enforcement was somehow an appropriate antidote to the city's social ills. Then and now, the facts about mass incarceration, policing, and crime can often be counterintuitive. Data on recidivism, the movement to privatize prisons, and the idea that substance abuse should be treated as a public health issue (rather than a criminal justice issue) all were available decades ago, but these ideas were not necessarily a feature of conventional thinking amidst the drug/crime hysteria in the era of crack cocaine.

And here is one of the inherent ironies of the Prison Industrial Complex: It can be all around us, and we can intuitively support the policies that make it

1

possible, and yet we may not know all of its deleterious effects on the communities that are most directly impacted by it.

Prison Industrial Complex For Beginners is an attempt to demystify the social ironies and brutal outcomes of various government policies—privatization, post-industrialism and the loss of jobs, the War on Drugs, mass incarceration—and to introduce and briefly explain how these policies inform what's known as the Prison Industrial Complex (PIC). If demystifying the PIC is a goal of this introductory project, then my hope is that what follows in the upcoming pages—both in narrative and in imagery—will help to unveil for all readers the urgency with which our society must approach the fact that the United States has the highest per-capita rate of incarceration of any of the so-called developed nations in the world.

Per-Capita Punishment

That awesome fact—*the United States incarcerates more people than any other nation in the world*—requires all American citizens to ask: Why are we the Incarceration Nation, and how did we become what we are today?

Prison Industrial Complex For Beginners attempts to answer these questions and provide some basic insights into the longer history that has shaped our strikingly excessive incarceration levels. The incarceration rate in a given nation (or state) is commonly defined as the number of prisoners per 100,000 members of the population. For "developed" nations comparable to the United States, the number tends to hover around **100** prisoners per 100,000 people. By contrast, the United States had a rate of **690**

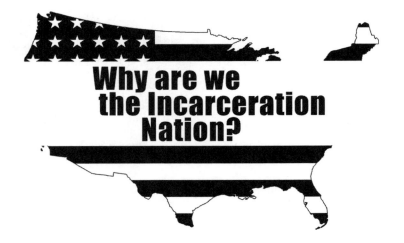

Why are we the Incarceration Nation?

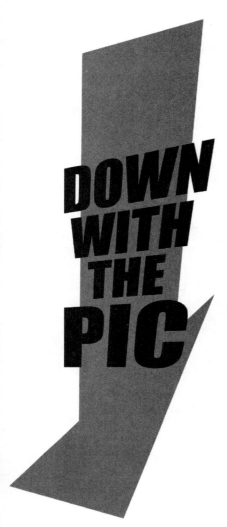

prisoners per 100,000 population in 2014, according to the Bureau of Justice Statistics. That came to a total of more than **2.2 million prisoners**. (Note: BJS *incarceration* figures include all inmates under the jurisdiction of state or federal prisons, as well as inmates held in city or county jails. *Imprisonment* rates and totals, another set of statistics reported by the Bureau, describes only the prison population under state or federal jurisdiction and sentenced to more than one year; these figures exclude unsentenced prisoners, those serving less than one year, and those held in local jails. The U.S. imprisonment total for 2014 came to 1.5 million, or a rate of 470 per 100,000 population.)

The United States does not lead the world in quality of public education, access to health care, life expectancy, or many of the other social metrics that matter to its citizens. Do we as a nation really want to be the number one incarcerator in the world?

No Joking Matter

One thing that national per-capita incarceration rates tend to mask is variation by state and region. Some states are worse offenders than others, incarcerating more than their share of citizens who enter the criminal justice system. As I have spent much of my adult life pursuing a graduate degree and working in the state of Pennsylvania, it is there that I have come of age (so to speak) with respect to my understanding of the Prison Industrial Complex. The second of my three academic jobs in Pennsylvania was located in the central region of the state. At an academic cocktail party not long after arriving there, a colleague proceeded to tell me a "joke." It went like this:

"What county in the state of Pennsylvania has the highest per-capita percentage of black males in its population?" he asked.

"Philadelphia County," I replied instantly, knowing that the county includes the city of Philadelphia, which has the largest black population in the state.

"Nope," he said.

So then I thought maybe the county where Pittsburgh was located had some dense underground population of black folks of which I was unaware.

"Allegheny County?" I guessed.

Again he said no.

Having lived and worked in Pennsylvania for some time, I was familiar with another old joke about the state—that politically and socially it was like New York (Philadelphia) at one end and Los Angeles (Pittsburgh) at the either end, with Alabama in between. But for the life of me, I could not figure out the riddle of this joke.

My colleague finally replied that the county we were in—Union County, in the largely rural central part of the state—had the highest rate of black men of any county in Pennsylvania because of all the state and federal prisons located in it. He proceeded to name all of them.

As you might imagine, I did not find his "joke" very funny. In fact, it required a particular approach to the data for it even to make factual sense. The truth is, there were (and still are) far more black folks in Philadelphia County, located in the southeastern portion of Pennsylvania, than there are in any other region of the state. There are also far more black folks in Pittsburgh and Allegheny County than in any county in central Pennsylvania. But in terms of how we calculate incarceration rates—per capita of the total population—my collegial jokester was right. The county in which we both lived, for all its rural and suburban splendor, housed several prison facilities that boosted the rate of black males in the overall population well beyond the region's general demographic profile.

Harsh Reality, Stark Truth

It was at this moment that I decided to visit and/or volunteer in as many of these facilities as I possibly could during my stay in central PA. And I did. I spent time at the Lewisburg Federal Penitentiary just as it was transitioning into a Supermax (super-maximum security) facility. I volunteered at the Federal Correctional Complex

in Allenwood, as well as other institutions/ facilities in the region. I did most of my volunteer work at the juvenile detention facility in Danville, PA.

What I found would not surprise any activist engaged in the battle to reform or revolutionize the American prison system. I cannot overstate the distinction between donating time to those incarcerated in our penal system versus those who actually have to "do" time in the system. There is no feeling quite like entering a prison, being searched, going through the metal detectors, and having a series of doors shut and locked

5

behind you. But I was always able to leave within a few hours. Donating time to folks on the "inside" is an important form of activism in the fight to bring our PIC to heel, but *doing* time on the "inside" is a radically different experience. Few people who have not been incarcerated can even begin to imagine what it's like.

What I found in my experiences at the Danville Juvenile Detention Center may not surprise any of the volunteers or activists reading this introduction to the PIC. The Danville facility was populated by a largely black and brown population of young men, many of them from Philadelphia. These young men were, by and large, engaging, intelligent, and, in some sad cases, consigned to their fate as property of the state. In 2002, when a group of Philadelphia rappers, including Beanie Sigel and the Young Guns, began to promote a brand

of clothing called State Property, detractors argued that the name suggested the very kind of attitude that led to the overrepresentation of young black men in state and federal correctional institutions.

This argument—much like the one that going to prison is a mere "rite of passage" for members of some communities—misses key points and ultimately ignores the systematic underpinnings of the Prison Industrial Complex. Young men and women from poor, underrepresented communities do not *aspire* to go to prison. They lack viable job opportunities and are assigned to underfunded, physically decrepit schools. In many cases, they have few options beyond the underground economies of their immediate environment. If black boys/men in any particular community are six times more likely to be incarcerated than their white counterparts (which they are), and if black people make up 13% of the U.S. population but more than 40% of the nation's prisoners (both of which are true), then certain cultural responses to institutional—and institutionally racist—phenomena will, of course, emerge.

Prison is *not* a rite of passage. It is a conventional reality of Black life in America, and it has been so since the end of slavery and ratification of the Thirteenth Amendment in 1865. "State Property" is a brand that the state itself created, not the Philadelphia rappers who tried to use it to draw attention to the fact that too many black youth are *actually* property of the state—even in the 21st century.

A Bow to Colleagues

The data on institutional biases in our criminal justice system and the Prison Industrial Complex are all quite clear and well quantified by activists and researchers who have focused on these issues for many years. In the midst of writing this book, I was invited to join a panel at the University of Virginia that featured some of these scholars, historians, and activists. Among them were Heather Ann Thompson (University of Michigan), Dennis Childs (University of California, San Diego), and Khalil Gibran Muhammad (Schomburg Center for Research in Black Culture). Much as I was excited to join such accomplished writers and thinkers committed to dismantling the Prison Industrial Complex, then, and now, I feel woefully unprepared to count myself among the scholars who do serious sustained work on the history of prisons and the Prison Industrial Complex.

Thompson's distillation of the problem in her award-wining 2010 article, "Why Mass Incarceration Matters," captures the issue and the critical incisiveness with which all of these scholars engage it.

> *Between 1970 and 2010 more people were incarcerated in the United States than were imprisoned in any other country, and at no other point in its past had the nation's economic, social, and political institutions become so bound up with the practice of punishment.*[1]

Throughout this volume, you will find that I rely heavily on the work of the thinkers, writers, and scholars who were present at the UVA gathering that day. Finding the balance between their work and writing a primer on the PIC has been one of the most difficult challenges of this project. But the role of writing in the construction of the PIC was historically vital, and my hope is that the role of writing—and drawing, in this case—will likewise contribute to the destruction of the Prison Industrial Complex.

Reading Khalil Gibran Muhammad's historical interpretation of *Race Traits and Tendencies of the American Negro,* by Frederick Ludwig Hoffman, still gives me the chills.[2] Hoffman was a Newark businessman who published the work in 1896, and it became one of the most influential race and crime studies ever to appear. It was said to be entirely objective, based solely on statistical data and written by someone who came from Germany whose research was uncontaminated by America's troubled history with race. Gibran argues convincingly to the contrary, forcing us to come to terms with the historical subjectivity of statistics and data. The fact is that the numbers we rely on for official "proof" of all things factual can, and have been, used in racist ways to undermine equality in America. Specifically, they influence Americans in the belief that

8

Black people are inherently criminal in nature. This is just one more long-running "joke" of the Prison Industrial Complex. As depicted in John Jennings's amazing cover art for this book, Black folks are believed to have an affinity for criminality *in utero*.

The work by scholars like Gibran, Thompson, Childs, Michelle Alexander, and Talitha LeFlouria is some of the most important in this field to date, especially with respect to the historical contours and continuities of violent Black oppression meted out by the state. At a meeting of the Association for the Study of African American Life and History (ASALH) in 2015, I had the unique opportunity to hear Professor Talitha LeFlouria's acceptance speech after winning a national book award from the organization for *Chained*

in Silence: Black Women and Convict Labor in the New South (2015). LeFlouria's book is an amazing historical chronicle of Black women who were exploited in the convict labor system—a thinly veiled front for the continuation of the American system of slavery and oppression after ratification of the Thirteenth Amendment. LeFlouria's speech at the conference was impassioned and unabashedly emotional, as she conveyed to the audience how deeply personal the work had become for her—how the stories of Black women conscripted to brutal labor conditions in the "New South" foretold the oppressive conditions of the PIC in contemporary society: Black women are the fastest growing demographic in the American prison system. Professor LeFlouria's tears compelled many in the audience to follow suit. For with knowledge of the long history of the Prison Industrial Complex comes both the frustration of perennial racialized oppression and the triumphant understanding of those who, throughout the course of American history, endured such oppression.

   *   *   *

 As much as possible, and in admittedly brief terms, I have tried to honor that history in the pages that follow. The opening chapter traces the history of the institution originally known as the "penitentiary" in the United States. Even that term—designating a place where penance might be achieved—belies the awful transition of the American prison system from its original purpose to its current status as a racially biased, privately influenced institution of (inhumane) human punishment. In the following chapters, I introduce the major components of the Prison Industrial Complex and the policies that have contributed to it. These include discussions of the War on Drugs, institutional and historical racism, privatization, and recidivism. Another important chapter introduces the specific issues of youth incarceration, the effects of U.S. immigration policies on incarceration, and the tragic consequences of solitary confinement.

In the end, this collection of topical inputs to the PIC can serve only as a rudimentary introduction for one of the most enduring and complicated social systems in American society. I can only hope that this introduction, in conjunction with the work of the aforementioned scholars and so many others referenced throughout, will provide a useful roadmap for any readers who might be interested in diving deeper into these and related issues to better understand—and begin dismantling—the Prison Industrial Complex in America.

Chapter 1
The Origin of Complexes

The Prison Industrial Complex (PIC) is the collection of social structures, systems, and policies—including institutional racism, the War on Drugs, and mass incarceration—that work together to confine and imprison more than 2 million American citizens. The United States incarcerates more of its citizens than any other "developed" nation in the world.

The PIC is a partnership that was nicknamed the "iron triangle" in the 1996 Report of the National Criminal Justice Commission.[3] It is a complicated and sometimes conspiratorial relationship between the government, private industries, lobbyists, and politicians that has been operating since the 1970s. Although reform efforts are starting to gain ground, the effects and consequences of the Prison Industrial Complex will be felt for many generations to come.

History

The U.S. penal system wasn't always this way. From the beginning of the nation's history (setting aside chattel slavery for the moment), and through much of the 18th century, jails in America were used for individuals who were in debt and/or awaiting trial.[4] For the most part, crime was deterred through debtor's jail, public lashings, bondage, and capital punishment; the death penalty was doled out for burglary and theft as well as murder. In the early days of the republic, the threat of being banished from the country or of being abandoned in the American wilderness was thought to be effective enough at deterring the nation's crime. Throughout the 18th century as well, jails and punishment were strategically employed to manage criminal behavior. As the nation grew in size, demographics, and scope, however, the challenge of controlling crime became a central feature of public and political discourse. So much so, that political thinkers began to ponder if an open and free society, like the fledgling United States, might in some ways facilitate criminal behavior as opposed to curtailing it.

In the early 19th century, therefore, the notion that criminals

could be reformed or rehabilitated took central stage in the American discourse on criminal justice. The nation's first prison systems were the structural results of that discourse—public conversations that wrestled with ways that society might rehabilitate criminals, viewed at the time as citizens who lacked discipline and had lost their way. The reliance on capital punishment and absence of many other alternatives for managing serious criminal behavior in a civil manner created a broad consensus on the need for new methods and new structures for the express purpose of housing and reforming criminals.

The flurry of public debates, pamphlets, and newspaper editorials soon focused on what kind of institution should be the model for America's prison system. The earliest debates revolved around two fairly similar prison systems planned for construction in the 1820s—one in New York according to the "Auburn" model, and the other in Philadelphia based on the "Pennsylvania" model.[5] The "Auburn" system versus the "Pennsylvania" system was one of the most intensely debated political and social issues of the 19th-century in America. "If the literature on Auburn versus Pennsylvania never quite matched the outpouring of material on the pros and cons of slavery," historians Norval Morris and David Rothman have written, "it came remarkably close."[6]

Prison Models

The Auburn model, which originated at upstate Auburn State Prison and then at Sing Sing along the Hudson River near New York City, was based on the "congregate" system of incarceration.[7] The congregate system, unlike the Pennsylvania system, allowed for some contact between prisoners. Because it did not require the

15

isolation of all prisoners in a given institution, the congregate (Auburn) system was more practical than the Pennsylvania system. It was also more affordable and, for the most part, more manageable for the institution.

For these reasons, the Auburn/congregate system became a pervasive model for prisons across the United States. In the 1820s, Connecticut, Maryland, and Massachusetts built and ran state prisons; Ohio, New Jersey, and Michigan added state prisons of their own in the 1830s; and in the 1840s, Minnesota, Indiana, and Wisconsin also followed suit.[8] Nearly all of these facilities employed the Auburn model.

Despite the dominance of congregate incarceration, it raised a number of logistical concerns for the early American carceral state—such as disciplinary techniques, prison garb, and the mobility of prisoners. All of these issues presented systemic challenges to the nation's emerging prison system.[9] Although chain gangs and guillotines were certainly cheaper than the huge superstructures that were becoming features of modern American society, the leadership class of the United States believed that the Auburn/congregation system was an altruistic advance in the human project. Prison reformers, by contrast, believed that efforts to construct a system of *penitentiaries* across the nation not only would address problems inside the institutions but could also solve problems outside the penal system, in the society at large. "With no ironies intended," write Morris and Rothman, "they talked about the penitentiary as serving as a model for the family and the school."[10]

Dawn of the Penitentiary

And so, in 1829, Quakers and other reformers in Philadelphia, Pennsylvania, followed a new and different philosophy in opening the Eastern State Penitentiary (ESP), occupying a full city block in the heart of the city.

Although most criminal justice scholars think of the Prison Industrial Complex as a modern phenomenon, dating to the 1970s, the birth of the penitentiary system sowed seeds of the PIC a century and a half before. The Eastern State Penitentiary was a state-of-the-art facility at the time of its opening. Its proponents asserted the viability of the Pennsylvania system of incarceration even as the Auburn system continued to attract its own political and ideological supporters. Although both systems relied on confinement, silence, and hard labor, the Pennsylvania system was based on solitary confinement as an exclusive form of incarceration and rehabilitation.[11] The Auburn system focused on unpaid (i.e., slave) labor by groups of prisoners, but it did allow inmates to come into contact with each other at certain times and locations, such as gathering for meals. But in the Pennsylvanian prison, according to theorist and prison historian Michel Foucault, "the only operations of correction were the conscience and the silent architecture that confronted it."[12]

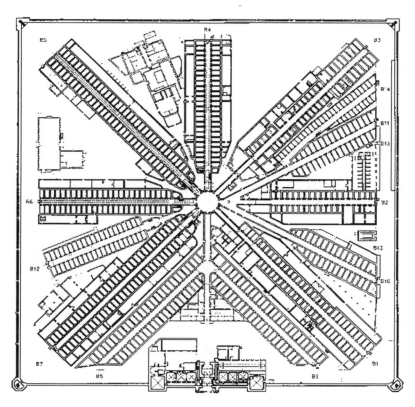

The architects of the world's first institutional prisons believed in solitary confinement as a form of penitence. Isolation, they contended, provided the space and time to reflect and consider God's judgment. Each cell in the ESP thus required prisoners to bow when entering and exiting; each cell was equipped with a small window sometimes referred to as "The Eye of God."

The Pennsylvania camp saw itself as purist, taking the idea of reform through isolation to its logical conclusion. It separated inmates from each other—to the point of placing hoods over the heads of newcomers so that as they walked to their cells they would not see or be seen by anyone.[13]

In a contemporary context, with horror stories like that of Kalief Browder—the New York 16-year-old who was arrested on robbery charges in 2010, held in solitary confinement for years without a trial, and eventually committed suicide—the idea of inmate isolation as a viable form of state-sanctioned imprisonment has come under severe criticism. But more on that later.

In the early to mid-19th century, the emphasis on solitary confinement and moral redemption embodied in the Pennsylvania system became a national and then global model for incarceration. Hundreds of prisons around the world came to be modeled after the Eastern State Penitentiary. This phenomenon— the influence of the Pennsylvania philosophy on the development of prisons around the world— foreshadowed a sort of complex within the Prison  Industrial Complex itself. That is, political leaders, partnerships between public and private enterprises, and the powerful influence of the burgeoning institutional model on the development of prisons, globally signaled a capacity to determine society's sense of what prisons should do and be. The American prison model would ultimately occupy a powerful space in the global social contract. According to one critic of the prison/crime industry, Nils Christie, contemporary "American criminology rules much of the world, their theories rule much of the world, their theories on crime and crime control exert enormous influence."[14]

The central idea of the Pennsylvania system was that reforming criminals in isolation was both possible and more useful to the greater societal good than simply punishing and/or killing them. The fact that this debate, with its deep philosophical questions regarding the purpose of prisons, was situated in the very origins of the American penal institution hints at some of the complexities of the current system.

The Eastern State Penitentiary operated from 1829 until 1971. Although the solitary penitent model failed by 1913, primarily because of capacity limitations, the reputation of the United States as a global leader in what Nils Christie defines as the "crime control industry" was already firmly established. The United States has remained a global leader in the building of prisons for nearly 200 years.

One of the most striking aspects of the American penitentiary system, present in both the Auburn and Pennsylvania models but most pronounced in the latter, was the pervasive and almost absolute silence of the institutions. Inspired by the reflective nature of Quaker meeting practices, the architects of the ESP believed in quiet as one way to reform society's wrongdoers. For them, silence was golden.

State-of-the-Art Prisons

It's important to note here that ESP was considered state of the art for its time—not just in terms of its awesome physical dimensions (30-foot walls, 27-foot oak doors, and an 80-foot bell tower)—but because it was an architectural and engineering wonder. The construction of ESP began in 1821 and was completed in 1829. It had running water some four years before the White House, considered essential to preserving the solitude and silence of each prisoner. The facility also featured a basic heating system, an amenity that many American citizens outside of prison could not afford.

Such advances presaged some of the ways that structural design and technological enhancements would continue to be a feature of the Prison Industrial Complex. In other words,

the faith that early American citizens placed (or misplaced, as it were) in the prison or penitentiary system was reflected in the nation's ideological, political, social, and financial investments in the institution itself. These investments often obscured Americans' ability to see just how horrific the prison system was in the 19th century, much as our current investments in the crime-control industry may be preventing us from seeing how horrific the prison system continues to be in the 21st century. Put another way, the amazing structure that the ESP became represented a socioeconomic and political symbol of the national commitment to using punishment as a means of reform and of making our wayward citizens penitent.

Prison design has become a permanently valuable aspect of the ongoing movement to construct prisons. According to journalist David Kidd,

> the design feature [of the ESP] that got the most attention was the cellblocks. Seven wings radiated out from a central open rotunda, allowing one guard to oversee the entire prison from a single spot. Today more than 300 prisons worldwide have a similar design, directly attributable to Eastern State's influence.[15]

Michel Foucault famously referred to this type of institutional building a *panopticon*. A structure that allowed just one guard to keep watch over hundreds of prisoner, the panopticon was an early form of surveillance that anticipated the role that technological surveillance plays in society today.

What *is* a Complex?

The phrase "industrial complex" was coined in a different context and some years before the rise of the PIC. It was first used in reference to the unchecked growth of the national defense budget and the concomitant privatization (and outsourcing) of military contracts. President Dwight Eisenhower, the great military leader of World War II, urged caution against the "military-industrial complex" in his farewell address to the nation on January 17, 1961. "We have been compelled to create a permanent armaments industry of vast proportions," Eisenhower warned. "In the councils of government," he went on,

we must guard against the acquisition of unwarranted influence, whether sought or unsought, by the military-industrial complex. The potential for the disastrous rise of misplaced power exists and will persist. We must never let the weight of this combination endanger our liberties or democratic processes.

For President Eisenhower, the military-industrial complex loomed large in the political, economic, and social future of America. The growing interface between privatization, militarization, and the prospect of permanent warfare was a serious concern.

*   *   *

The term "prison industrial complex" entered the public discourse by way of Mike Davis's article in *The Nation* on February 20, 1995, titled "Hell Factories in the Field: A Prison-Industrial Complex." The "hell factories" referred to in that groundbreaking article were the 16 prisons built over the course of the previous decade in the state of California. The term "field" refers both to the rural regions of the state that were ideal locations for the development of California's PIC and to Davis's recognition of the extraordinary growth—and capacity for continued growth—of the complex itself.

That expansion of the PIC, according to activist-scholar Angela Davis (no relation to Mike), had "already begun in the 1990s to

rival agribusiness and land development as a major economic and political force."[16] If the PIC in a state as large as California—often regarded as a bellwether of social change for the rest of the nation—was showing signs of the kind of influence over the political economy that agriculture or "agribusiness" had already established, then in many ways the writing was on the wall.

Like the military-industrial complex and agribusiness, multibillion-dollar industries subsidized by the U.S. government, the PIC soon had its own lobbyists, direct connections to the captains of industry, and elected political leaders at every level of government with interests across multiple private industries. As Mike Davis wrote in "Hell Factories," the PIC

> *has become a monster that threatens to overpower and devour its creators, and its uncontrollable growth ought to rattle a national consciousness now complacent at the thought of a permanent prison class.*[17]

The Uncontrollable Monster

In order to understand how this uncontrollable monster came into prominence during the latter half of the 20th century, we need to look at several of the PIC's fundamental driving forces. Some of these will be briefly detailed here, while others, warranting more time and attention, will be taken up in subsequent chapters.

The fear of crime, especially violent crime, has tremendous political and economic capital in the United States. Even though violent crime has dropped precipitously and consistently since the 1990s—the same decade that expanded the modern-day Prison Industrial Complex—media reporting of violent crime has continued to increase, by some estimates five-fold or 500 percent since the 1990s. More importantly, surveys showed, the American people believed that crime was still a major problem even as criminal activity continued to decline in the last days of the millennium.[18]

This suggests a critical phenomenon from a political perspective. If citizens' concerns about crime can be stoked by the media, and if those concerns persist despite falling crime rates, then political leaders will always find incentives for being "tough on crime." Beyond the political efficacy of exploiting constituents' fears for the purpose of eliciting votes, an inordinate public fear of crime creates an environment that forecloses progress and cultivates a political system vulnerable to corruption. Since "politicians in both parties and all levels of government have used fear of crime to generate votes," how can we be sure that the peoples' political interests are being served by decisions (or deals) made by political leaders when it comes to addressing the problems of crime in our society? [19]

If the fear of crime creates tremendous political capital, then the industry of crime control engenders tremendous *monetary* capital. At the dawn of the PIC, approximately $100 billion was being spent on law enforcement annually in the United States.[20] According to President Barack Obama in his July 2015 speech on mass incarceration speech, the nation at that time was spending $80 billion a year to lead the world in incarceration. This does not even include the money spent on private security ($65 billion annually) or the web of corporate tentacles that extend from the PIC into the economy at large—such as food services, construction, and telephone/wireless services.

MIC Meets PIC

One of the less visible but more egregious examples of the "industry" aspect of the PIC is the interface between military technologies and the crime-control industry itself—where the MIC and PIC meet. This intersection highlights some of the most compelling arguments for dismantling or comprehensively overhauling the PIC.

While the American public and its local communities remain highly interested and heavily invested in public safety, private industries are mostly concerned with profits and "bottom lines." In "Fear, Politics, and The Prison Industrial Complex," a section from the 1996 report of the National Criminal Justice Commission, the disconnection between public safety and private interests comes into sharp focus. At national conventions and trade shows, companies that produce military technology for U.S. armed forces during times of war now market their products to the PIC. All sorts of surveillance technology—listening and viewing devices, lethal and nonlethal weapons, and all sorts of innovative gear and equipment—are on display and pitched to the American prison industries.

Military technology is not the only industry that profits from the PIC. Any number of other private-sector concerns provide services to the PIC, including but not limited to food services, transportation services, medical services, waste management, drug testing/treatment, and one of the most exploitative industries profiting from the system: cell phone service. Prisons in America are big business, and private industry realized this three decades ago.

Consider also the fact that any economic interaction between the MIC and the PIC, or between consumer product/service corporations and the PIC, creates enormous opportunity for employment. In the early 1990s, the PIC employed more than 500,000 correctional officers and other correctional facility personnel—a significant portion of the total U.S. workforce. Considered in the context of the wide-ranging employment opportunities and contract work associated with the PIC, the economic depth and breadth of the complex becomes clear and compelling. In many communities, especially rural ones, the

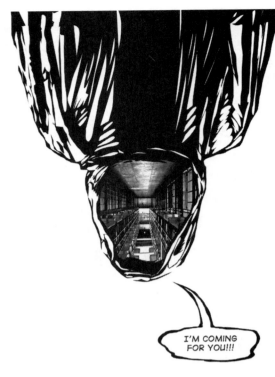

I'M COMING FOR YOU!!!

possibility of building and operating a prison in the region is an economic offer that political leaders cannot refuse. The entire economy of certain communities revolves around a local manifestation of the PIC.

The Specter of Prisons

In the early 21st century, the PIC is a prominent feature of the world in which we live. In their book *Beyond the Prison Industrial Complex* (2013), Kevin Wehr and Elyshia Aseltine warn that "[t]he specter of the prison is all around: police cars, surveillance cameras, signs warning that shoplifters will be prosecuted."[21] The visible and tangible signs of the Prison Industrial Complex are ubiquitous. For Wehr and Aseltine, these signs declare an implied "or else" that threatens incarceration at multiple points and places throughout American society—especially where poor people of color live and move.

Those threats represent a social failing of sorts, given that "[w]e have known since the 1830s that prisons do not reduce crime."[22] Yet our reliance on the Prison Industrial Complex continues to defy social science logic and the data that continues to undermine the basic premises of incarceration: deterrence and rehabilitation. What the PIC is best at is retribution, sometimes in the form of sentences and diminished quality of life that expose the state as a biased, vengeful actor against humanity.

The contemporary PIC, then, is very much a consequence of neoliberalism and global capitalism—that is, a complex designed to serve an economic system that must account for expanding income inequality and unemployment. In the United States, the PIC accounts for such shifts in the political economy with explicit and implicit biases leveraged against poor people, women, and people of color. And the effects have been devastating. The United States accounts for about 5% of the world's population and 25% of the world's prison population. At the height of the PIC in 2006, the United States incarcerated some 2.5 million people—more than the population of such major cities as Dallas, Philadelphia, and San Francisco.

From School to Prison

The slight decline from 2.5 million to 2.2 million incarcerated in recent years is not from lack of trying. One feature of the Prison Industrial Complex is the "school-to-prison pipeline," a phrase that captured the unfortunate correlations between the social, educational, and financial erosion of the nation's public education system and the growth of the PIC. What happens when the profit motives of the PIC work in concert with the persistent, systemic undervaluation of public education?

Consider the effects of school closings in cities like Chicago, New York, and Philadelphia. In 2010–2011, nearly 100 public school closings in those three cities impacted between 82% and 94% of

low-income students. In Philly and Chicago, black students were especially hard hit—81% and 88%, respectively.[23] Statistics and news accounts of a public school closing cannot begin to convey the dramatic impact on a neighborhood or community. At their best, public school buildings are institutional outposts of municipal support in urban deserts overwrought by concentrated poverty.

The closing of public schools, especially in the face of increased funding for jails and prisons, puts into stark relief the value judgments of American society with regard to education and incarceration. While it cost approximately

$11,000 a year to educate a young person in the United States today, it costs about $90,000 to house one of them in the PIC. During the 20-year period from the mid-1990s to the mid-2010s, PIC funding increased 530% more than educational funding. Data such as these, and the day-to-day realities that underlie them, reveal the irrational and discriminatory nature of the "tough on crime" ethos that pro-prison advocates use to hide or obscure the actual issues that drive the PIC. The expansion of the prison system occurs over and above any serious political consideration of the complex's deleterious and racially disparate consequences on the poor and mentally ill.

The facts do not overstate the profitability of America's $80 billion Prison Industrial Complex. Sadly, profitability in the prison industries contaminates the American criminal justice system. In their book *Justice While Black* (2014), Robbin Shipp and Nick Chiles point to particularly egregious misuses of the criminal justice system for profit and discriminatory carceral practices.

> *In Wilkes-Barre, PA two judges pleaded guilty in 2009 to accepting 2.6 million in bribes in exchange for sending juvenile defendants to local, privately run facilities, regardless of whether they were guilty or innocent or how severe their supposed crimes were.*[24]

When judges collude with private facilities to access taxpayer dollars for their own personal profit, the system's complex nature and critical consequences become all the more clear. And the Wilkes-Barre model of the complex is not unique. In municipalities like

Meridian, MS, and Ferguson, MO, the organized and sometimes illegal interface between the government, private industry, and law enforcement is one of the most effective forms of racial discrimination since the transatlantic slave trade.

Understanding the long history of prisons and the full definition of the Prison Industrial Complex should be a required feature of public education in America. Given the sad correlation between incarceration and lack of education, teaching about the PIC in public schools might demonstrate to students both the value of educational attainment (by any means necessary) and the pitfalls of the criminal justice system in the 21st century. Equity, equality, and equal justice under the law are the predicates for U.S. citizenship without which we cannot become civically engaged in the political system. Given the ways that public education and criminal justice are linked in our nation, knowledge about the PIC might actually prevent some of our citizens from becoming subject to its often arbitrary and confining forces.

Chapter 2

Race and the Persistence of Law-and-Order Ideology

Standing in one of several dungeons in Cape Coast Castle, located on the Gulf of Guinea in Ghana, West Africa, a deeper understanding of the prehistoric nature of the role of racism in the world's prison systems becomes painfully apparent. Race, racism, and the lives of Africans and their diasporic descendants have been features of the earliest forms of what we refer to as the Prison Industrial Complex in the modern era.

Where to Begin?

Our historical concept of slavery often frames America as the brutal point of origin of the bondage, confinement, and forced labor that characterized the institution beginning in the 17th century. Some students, scholars, and historians situate that point of origin in the Middle Passage—the brutal journey across the Atlantic Ocean that millions of enslaved Africans, chained, confined, and tortured in the cramped hulls of transatlantic slave ships, were forced to endure. But before bondage, confinement, and force labor, before the genocidal journey of the Middle Passage, native Africans were detained, tortured, branded, and otherwise "processed" in fantastic colonial complexes—often referred to as "slave castles"— along the coast of western Africa.

Approximately 40% of all enslaved Africans who were

brutalized, shackled, and confined before the awful Middle Passage were processed through one of many slave castles along the coast of Ghana, historically known as the Gold Coast for its rich gold dust resources. Designed as military forts for the purpose of trade, the slave castles were soon repurposed and outfitted as dungeons and various slaveholding and/or detention facilities. The "door of no return," though which millions of Africans left their home continent from the slave castles, is a powerful symbol of the ways that the Black experience in the modern world is shaped and informed by the full range of systems, tools, and complexes designed to detain, dehumanize, torture, and incarcerate black bodies. These structures were, in fact, an important early component in a long, continuous history of the Prison Industrial Complex.

The slave castles of West Africa, like the penitentiaries of 19th-century America, had an imposing architecture: towers for surveillance; dungeons of various shapes, sizes, and purposes, some for the sole intent of confining and starving "unruly" Africans to death; as well as chapels for prayer and worship. Built within the confines of large colonial complexes, the slave castles represent the very essence and ethos of the modern-day Prison Industrial Complex. The partnerships in the era of the transatlantic slave trade included various colonial governments, the leadership of certain African tribes, the European and American shipping industries, and all of the private profiteers who benefitted directly from chattel slavery—including many of the "founding fathers" of the United States and all of the agricultural and manufacturing economies that benefitted from the labor of enslaved Africans.

Reviewing the history of the transatlantic slave trades is largely beyond the scope of this introduction to the PIC, but it is worth noting that what we refer to as the "complex" in this discussion has many antecedents in two-and-a-half centuries of American slavery. Forced labor, rampant rape, complete confinement, and systematic dehumanization—all for profit—are well-known features of both the historical institution of bondage and the contemporary institution known as the Prison Industrial Complex. Moreover, the fact that these institutions/complexes single out people of a darker hue is neither incidental nor accidental. These are institutions that together and throughout history have deliberately targeted people of color, poor folks, and especially Black folks.

The striking connections between the long, terrible history of the transatlantic slave trade and contemporary policies such as mass incarceration or institutions such as the Prison Industrial Complex

have been detailed by a wide array of scholars, including Michelle Alexander, Marc Mauer, Douglas Blackmon, Dennis Childs, Khalid Gibran Muhammad, Talitha LeFlouria, Heather Ann Thompson, and many more. What these scholars have very effectively done is identify the racist policies and institutions through which we can trace a history of the Prison Industrial Complex that begins in the slave castles of West Africa; that comes through the Middle Passage; that establishes itself as chattel slavery and bondage in the United States for hundreds of years; that transforms into policies such as the Black Laws, debt peonage, convict leasing, and chain gangs; and, in the post–Civil War era, that continues to feed black bodies and often enslaved labor through a growing prison system into the American industrial revolution. The partnership between policy makers, private industry, and the penal system—i.e., the complex—had been in place long before what we normally consider the origins of the modern PIC.

A deep historical understanding of the Prison Industrial Complex requires an understanding of the genesis of the transatlantic slave trade, especially the use of torture, branding, chains, and dungeons to dehumanize Africans (and their captors) at colonial slave castles. And after the Middle Passage, during which the same tactics were used,

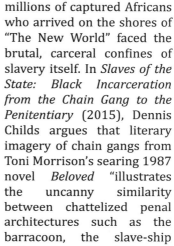

millions of captured Africans who arrived on the shores of "The New World" faced the brutal, carceral confines of slavery itself. In *Slaves of the State: Black Incarceration from the Chain Gang to the Penitentiary* (2015), Dennis Childs argues that literary imagery of chain gangs from Toni Morrison's searing 1987 novel *Beloved* "illustrates the uncanny similarity between chattelized penal architectures such as the barracoon, the slave-ship hold, the slave pen, the chain-gang cage, and the solitary-confinement cell."[25]

The slave castle can be added to this list as well. And note the historical continuity of these various penal structures. The barracoon (a word derived from the Spanish *barracon*) was a kind of barracks repurposed to hold slaves or convicts. On the continent of Africa, these "slave sheds" served brutal functions. Nineteenth-century author E. J. Glave explains:

At every village bands of slaves were offered for sale; it would be difficult to give a truthful picture of the suffering endured by captives . . . . They are hobbled with roughly hewn logs which chafe their limbs to open sores; sometimes a whole tree presses its weight on their bodies while their necks are penned . . . . Others sit from day to day with their legs and arms maintained in a fixed position by rudely constructed stocks, and each slave is secured to the roof-posts by a cord knotted to a cane ring which either encircles his neck or is intertwined with his woolly hair. Many die of pure starvation . . . .[26]

The Dirty Little Secret of the 13th Amendment

The physical conditions of enslaved Africans imprisoned in barracoons indicate the awful ways that violent dehumanization is an inherent feature of early forms of incarceration. More to the point in the present discussion, the same kind of confinement came to be imposed on convicts as on slaves. The infliction of such punishment on either slaves *or* prisoners highlights what many of the aforementioned scholars consider to be the dirty little secret of the Thirteenth Amendment. Officially ratified by the states on December 6, 1865, just months after the end of the Civil War, the Thirteenth Amendment declared slavery and involuntary servitude illegal across the nation:

> *Neither slavery nor involuntary servitude, except as a punishment for crime whereof the party shall have been duly convicted, shall exist within the United States, or any place subject to their jurisdiction.*

But the exception specified in the language is important to note in the present context. The fact that individuals duly convicted of a crime can be subject to involuntary labor or servitude meant literally that convicts were slaves of the state.

In contemporary times, some African American public figures and scholars have called for the designation of December 6 as a national holiday, to be called Abolition Day. As noted by many of the aforementioned scholars, however, the exception specified in Thirteenth Amendment—that convicted criminals can be subject to involuntary labor or servitude—left the door open for the cultural momentum to coalesce around several harsh responses, especially from white supremacists. This was especially true in the aftermath

ARTICLE XIII.

SECTION 1. Neither slavery nor involuntary servitude, **except as a punishment for crime whereof the party shall have been duly convicted,** shall exist within the United States, or any place subject to their jurisdiction.

SECTION 2. Congress shall have power to enforce this article by appropriate legislation.

APPROVED, February 1, 1865.

of the Civil War across the South, where the appetite for sustaining systemic racism was remained strong.

One of the outcomes of the convict exception clause and the intense hatred toward newly freed Blacks was the implementation of a series of laws and policies that centered on controlling and confining Black folks in public spaces. Many of these laws focused on vagrancy, and they came to be known as the Black Codes. They derived from the "slave codes" that had been put in place in the individual colonies and states in previous centuries to restrict the rights of slaves and to reaffirm the mastery of their owners.

Pre-PIC Policies

The **Black Codes** had been designed to limit the lives and freedom of Black people in the antebellum South. While they limited the rights of Blacks to conduct business and own property, some of the most pernicious codes were measures for patrolling (and controlling) them in public spaces. The central features of the Black Codes were a series of vagrancy laws implemented first in Mississippi and eventually throughout the Deep South in 1865–1866. These laws, devised and implemented just as enslaved Black folks were being officially liberated, quickly and efficiently ruled out the possibility of actual freedom for African Americans in the antebellum South. They also sowed the seeds for how incarceration policies could and would be racialized, and the ways in which forced labor and economic interests became features of the Prison Industrial Complex.

Debt peonage, also referred to as "debt servitude" or "debt slavery," was initially a legal process by which an employer could advance certain resources to an employee—such as travel costs or lodging—and the employee would then be compelled to "work off" the debt. The practice was outlawed in 1867, however, because the arrangement often proved detrimental to the "employee." Working off the debt in many cases amounted to long-term or permanent enslavement.

The most egregious abuses of the debt peonage system emerged from the confluence of the Black Codes and the residue of white supremacy in the South. Black men and women who were arrested for vagrancy, loitering, or not having a verifiable job were often charged egregious fines and court fees. When they were unable to pay, they were conscripted into a variety of forms of debt peonage in workplaces and labor situations determined by the state. Here again, the fundamental aspects of the modern Prison Industrial Complex and the stubbornness of American racism worked in tandem to confine, incarcerate, and exploit black folks.

In his groundbreaking book and documentary film, *Slavery by Another Name* (2008 and 2012), Douglas Blackmon chronicles the oppressive continuities between traditional slavery, debt peonage, convict leasing, and the chain gang.[27] **Convict leasing** is a particularly significant model to consider in the long history of the Prison Industrial Complex. One consequence of the Civil War

was that the infrastructure of the South was almost completely destroyed in many areas. Most of the prisons were destroyed, and lawlessness was generally on the rise. In order to address the lack of prisons, many Southern states outsourced convict housing to private entities. This was not the full-on privatization of prisons that we see in contemporary times, but it was definitely a precursor to the kinds of public-private partnerships through which the Prison Industrial Complex continues to thrive.

Within years of the private housing of prisoners in the South, some states opted to "lease" prisoners to private agricultural and industrial businesses, providing them with ultra-cheap labor. Unfortunately, the private entities had little or no financial incentive to treat convict-leased laborers with any sense of humanity, making many convict leasing programs inherently brutal and often deadly.

Although we often envision black men being subject to such historical atrocities, it is important to note that black women (albeit in a smaller percentage) were also subject to the inhumane practices of convict leasing in the South. Talitha LeFlouria's *Chained in Silence* chronicles the peculiar challenges of the "lived and laboring experiences" of the South's "most inconspicuous workforce—black convict women."[28]

Eventually, the abuse of both women and men in the convict leasing system led to the demise of these programs as standard practice. Rather than lease their enslaved labor to private corporations, states decided to keep their workforces "in-house." Thus was born the next iteration of the same phenomenon found throughout the long history of the PIC: **the chain gang**.

As public sensitivity to the perils of convict leasing became prevalent, chain gangs emerged as the contemporary iteration of PIC forces in the early years of the 20th century. Chain gangs are groups of convicts physically shackled together and forced to work on public projects, usually roads, railroads, construction projects, and/or agricultural sites. Convicts who worked in chain gangs were, not surprisingly, subject to extremely harsh treatment: long hours, physical punishment, and deplorable work conditions. What ultimately liberated the nation from this inhumane institution was the sheer physical damage that the chains themselves did to the bodies of the convicts. When the shackles came off, chain gangs became heavily guarded work gangs—a phenomenon still common in contemporary criminal justice.

The ultimate consequence of these sometimes hastily assembled partnerships among oppressors/former enslavers, private industries, and the government was a growing sense that criminality was inherently black. This, in turn, became a centerpiece of American criminal justice ideology. The aggressive nature through which the Black Codes produced convicts for private enslavement led to an abiding sense of the blackness of criminality and the perceived criminality inherent in blackness. Sadly, the residue of these sinister partnerships between the state, institutional racism, and private industries continues to inform mass-incarceration policies and the dominance of the Prison Industrial Complex in America today.

A Civil Rights Movement for the Ages

By the mid-twentieth century, many of the policies and capitalist incentives for debt peonage, convict leasing, and, to a lesser extent, chain gangs had begun to dissipate. Black folks were still disproportionately and disparately impacted by the U.S. criminal justice system, but a new movement emerged in force to address these and other issues of racial and social injustice. The Civil Rights

46

Movement, including civic action in the form of boycotts, sit-ins, freedom rides, and protest marches, as well as the government policies handed down in the *Brown v. Board of Education* decision (1954), the Civil Rights Act of 1964, and the Voting Rights Acts of 1965, all highlighted and directly addressed the historically persistent manifestations of anti-black racism in America. The movement's organizers and leaders understood explicitly the role that the police and the state had long played in the oppression and repression of black folks across the nation.

The Rev. Martin Luther King, Jr.'s iconic "Letter from a Birmingham Jail" in 1963 crystallizes the collective sensibility that confrontation with a racist police state, hateful whites, and the carceral spaces that shape the experiences of black folks under critical racial duress were vital components of the African American Civil Rights Movement. An exhaustive history of that movement is (also) beyond the purview of this introduction to the PIC, but some cursory notes on the response to the movement and the cultural and political climate that it created are central to understanding the long history of the Prison Industrial Complex.

The civil rights campaign of the 1950s and 1960s was one of the most legislatively successful movements in the nation's history. While it highlighted the stagnation of racial oppression from 1865 to 1965, it also achieved specific legal remedies for American racism. One of the more successful efforts of the movement was its peaceful

organization of multiple civic actions, which led to both peaceful and violent confrontations with law enforcement. But the movement was hardly without its limitations, its challenges, and its tragedies. The murder of several leaders of the movement fed the anxiety in American race relations, and at times civic resistance marches did not seem to be enough to contain the collective outrage. The combination of peaceful civic action and violent urban uprisings that developed largely in response to the murders of prominent Civil Rights leaders set yet another stage upon which the long history of the PIC would finally arrive in the modern era.

The Rise of Nixon and Law-and-Order Politics

Although the 1960s are often depicted as a time of great social and political change, a liberal moment in the political development of modern America, Republican Richard Nixon saw something different even in his early failings as an elected politician. Nixon lost a presidential bid in 1960 and a California gubernatorial election in 1962. Although he claimed that his loss in '62 signaled the end of his life in politics, it was really just the beginning. Nixon began to stump for a variety of GOP office-seekers across the spectrum, including candidates for the House and the Senate and Barry Goldwater in the 1964 presidential cycle. Although Goldwater lost in a landslide, many of the other candidates whom Nixon supported did win. Moreover, Nixon identified an abiding sentiment among white voters across the nation—an express desire for public "order."

The Nixon campaign embraced and promoted that desire in the slogan "law and order." In the 1968 presidential election, the phrase also turned out to be a winning strategy. The ideology of law and order was a political response to the civic unrest generated by the Civil Rights and anti–Vietnam War movements of the 1960s. It was predicated on the sense that those "radical" movements had undermined the ethical fabric of the American project.

In the years and decades that followed, law and order became a permanent feature of American politics—an abiding conviction in some circles that order must be sustained through law enforcement and incarceration, and that no other remedies are available to citizens or the government to address civic unrest, criminal behavior, drug addiction, and a whole range of other social issues.

Yet in order for law and order to become the order of the day, certain social developments and public discourses already had to have been in play. According to criminal justice expert Marc Mauer,

"the race to incarcerate" began during President Nixon's second term in 1973, but the discourses that informed that phenomenon had been taking place since the 1960s. While American prisons had not changed much since the founding of the Eastern State Penitentiary in 1829, the question of the prison's social purpose was again being vigorously debated. The central issue during the 1960s was whether the prison served the primary purpose of rehabilitating prisoners or of deterring *potential* criminals from committing crimes at all. "In 1968, 72% of Americans told pollsters the goal of the prison should be rehabilitation."[29]

That sentiment obscured the critical debate between policy advocates on the left and the right. Leftist thinkers at the time questioned the ability of prisons to rehabilitate prisoners through confinement and coercion. They also pointed to social issues such as poverty and lack of education as the structural causes of society's criminality problems. Conservative thinkers, to the contrary, argued that crime was on the rise as a result of a weakened criminal justice system and the leniency of liberal activists. Ultimately they also rejected the possibility of rehabilitation. For conservatives, the prison system's purpose was to punish criminals and keep them off of the streets of America. The conservatives ultimately "won" this sociopolitical debate, at least in part due to a popular study of studies published by sociologist Robert Martinson in 1974.

Nothing Works

Over the course of the long history of prisons in America, several articles and books have had an outsized impact on incarceration policy. Martinson's 1974 study, "What Works: Questions and Answers About Prison Reform" was certainly one of the most influential articles published on prisons, prison reform efforts, and criminal justice policy in the United States. In the article, Martinson details his and his collaborators' assessments of more than 200 prison rehabilitation and/or recidivism studies. "[Recidivism can be defined as the rate at which released or paroled prisoners return to prison for additional crimes.)

Martinson's conclusions were dire in terms of the possibility that *any* approach to reforming criminals (at least to that point) actually had a positive effect. In short, "What Works" examined a broad range of reforms that, according to Martinson, didn't work at all. Some of the studies debunked by Martinson included support for the following types of reforms: group counseling, reduced sentencing, more humane institutional environments, medical treatment (including drug/tranquilizer therapy and/or surgery), decarceration, community treatment, intensive supervision for youthful and adult offenders, probation, parole, and psychotherapy. "I am bound to say," Martinson wrote,

> *that these data, involving over two hundred studies and hundreds of thousands of individuals ... are the best available and give us very little reason to hope that we have in fact found a sure way of reducing recidivism through rehabilitation."[30]*

Aside from the apparent comprehensiveness of the study, the idea that Martinson attacked "hope" itself is telling. Indeed it had a devastating effect on people's belief in rehabilitation. The idea that "nothing works" when it came to criminality and incarceration struck a chord with an American mainstream haunted by the specter of black civic unrest, which it perceived as little more than lawlessness. And the "nothing works" doctrine was also embraced by politicians committed to law and order by any means necessary. Martinson went a step further in his conclusion about American society, pointing to *a more radical flaw in our present strategies—that education at its best, or that psychotherapy at its best, cannot overcome, or even appreciably reduce, the powerful tendency for offenders to continue in criminal behavior.[31]*

The implications of this "flaw" in terms of the ways policy makers would think about drug addiction, poverty, and the role of public education in deterring crime has remained powerfully influential since 1974. That is, the ways in which policies like mass incarceration and the forging of partnerships that produce the Prison Industrial Complex have been able to thrive since the 1970s reflects the same lack of hope in human redemption and the same acceptance of the "nothing works" view of progressive strategies like access to public education and professional treatment for people with mental illnesses. The data is clear that the American prison population today is woefully undereducated and that we have been warehousing rather than treating the mentally ill within the Prison Industrial Complex for decades.

A great many researchers and scholars have debunked Martinson's claims in "What Works"—he himself recanted years later—but the damage had been done. Nothing he ever published proved as popular, as widely read, or as influential on public policy as his grim assessment of criminal rehabilitation. One of the ironies of Martinson's life is that he was a liberal/progressive activist in his youth. Born in Minneapolis in 1927, he attended the University of California, Berkeley, and ran for mayor of that city as a member of the Socialist Party in 1959. Two years later, he actually spent time in two Mississippi jails for his participation in the Freedom Rides (the civil

rights campaign to challenge non-enforcement of desegregation laws on public buses in the South). While that incarceration sparked his interest in criminal justice, Martinson became part of the very social movement that produced the public appetite for law and order in the first place.

Race, Law and Order

Taken out of historical context, the ideology of law and order in contemporary American society seems innocuous, even mandatory. Of course citizens of a civilized society want law and order! Society requires rules and laws in order to sustain itself. People who commit crimes should be subjected to an unbiased criminal justice system that fairly and humanely works to mete out justice relative to the criminal activity in question.

In the historical context of the Prison Industrial Complex, however, the phrase "law and order" points to a more complicated understanding of the social forces at work in American criminal justice. The contemporary notion of law order is ideologically rooted in racist sentiments regarding the efforts and accomplishments of the Civil Rights Movement, and an abiding mainstream fear that black folks might take their urban uprisings to the next level—i.e., full-blown REVOLUTION.

That relatively recent history is further buttressed by the long history of the Prison Industrial Complex—a legacy that begins with the transatlantic slave trade. To say that Black people came

to America in chains does not fully capture the economic and institutional forces at work at the very dawn of the nation in terms of the confinement, enslavement, and exploitation of Black people that would persist for centuries. The long history of the Prison Industrial Complex also highlights the incredible work done by contemporary prison studies scholars who have excavated the ongoing histories of collusion between private industry and government under the umbrella of white supremacy and anti-black racism—the very substance of our contemporary penal complex. Race/racism and the conceptualization of law and order as we know it are inextricably linked elements of the PIC. Without them, the complex as we know it today could not exist.

Chapter 3

The Failed War(s) on Drugs

In 2004, while running for a U.S. Senate seat from Illinois, candidate Barack Obama made the following blunt statement: "The war on drugs has been an utter failure."

He was correct in many ways.

The War on Drugs had been declared by President Richard Nixon in a message to Congress in June 1971. The first major salvo was the Comprehensive Drug Abuse Prevention and Control Act, which designated five "schedules" (or classes) of controlled substances and penalties for their abuse. Schedule I drugs (including marijuana, heroin, and cocaine) required stricter regulation and penalties than Schedule II drugs (codeine, morphine, and others); Schedule III drugs (including anabolic steroids and LSD); Schedule IV drugs (including a number of stimulants and depressants); and Schedule V drugs (such as codeine or opium). The legislation targeted the pharmaceutical industry, requiring better security and a more comprehensive accounting system for how drugs were disseminated.

Since implementation of the first drug-war initiatives, the U.S. government has spent over $1.5 trillion on drug regulation and drug-related law enforcement. Over the same period of time, however, the nation's drug addiction rates have remained relatively consistent.

And while rates of drug addiction have remained largely unchanged, the Prison Industrial Complex has thrived: the number of people incarcerated in the United States has increased exponentially over the same period. Given the unconscionable amount of money and resources spent on a "war" with negligible impact on the "enemy," it's fair to say that candidate Obama was right: the War on Drugs has been an abject failure.

That said, it's also important to note that there are shades to this failure—a range of unintended and intended consequences evident at the intersections of the Prison Industrial Complex and U.S. drug policy.

Race and a History of Drug Policy

The War on Drugs, not unlike the PIC, has a long racialized history that is worth considering alongside the deeply racialized consequences of mass incarceration. Historically, U.S. policy on illegal drugs repeatedly has been driven by ideologies that center on racist messaging pegged to particular groups of recent immigrant. In the mid-19th century, for example, with the influx of Chinese immigrants arriving in the West, virulent anti-Chinese propaganda gave rise to California drug laws—the first in the country—targeting opium. In the early 20th century, laws designed to regulate cocaine were fueled by racialized propaganda  centered on menacing African American men. And the earliest laws designed to restrict and/or outlaw marijuana emerged in response to anti-Mexican and Mexican American sentiments in the West and Southwest.[32] The closely intertwined history of drug policy, race, and racist propaganda in America is long and sad, with thousands upon thousands of people imprisoned and very little understood about

drug abuse as a public health issue.

Recreational drug use emerged in the United States in the first half of the 19th century. Opium became more popular during the Civil War era. And by the late 19th century, cocaine and coca were being touted as tonics and used in soft drinks and other consumer products.[33] Eventually, the medical community recognized that many psychoactive drugs were physically and/or psychologically addictive—thus began the country's commitment to demonizing drug addicts and substance abusers.

Data on drug addiction clearly indicate that the decades-long War on Drugs has been ineffectual in both stemming the demand and stopping the supply of controlled substances in the United States. Instead, what the war *has been* extremely effective at is generating policies that lead to incarceration. According to social justice activist James Kilgore,

prosecution of drug cases has stood at the heart of both the expansion of the prison population and the philosophical shift to a more punitive system since the late 1970s.[34]

57

Many of the early antidrug measures in America focused on control and/or regulation of the substances themselves. The Harrison Narcotics Act of 1914, for example, was designed to control the processing and distribution of marijuana and cocaine. But that legislation tended to focus on penalizing physicians in an attempt to change the culture of healthcare; many believed that doctors were stringing along drug addicts in much the same ways that we think of illegal drug dealers stringing along helplessly addicted heroin or crack users.

There is much to be said (and researched) regarding the persistence of this aspect of doctor-patient culture at a moment when pharmaceutical corporations advertise "legal" drugs on television, online, and elsewhere in the media with seemingly reckless abandon. Then again, over the long arc of history, U.S. drug policy seems to move unidirectionally toward penalizing addicts rather than treating them, and toward the incarceration of illegal substance users rather than developing objective policies that make sense in a society in which drugs (legal and illegal) are a ubiquitous feature.

The aftermath of the Harrison Act, which by some estimates led to the incarceration of several thousand doctor-dealers, brought a long onslaught of legislation and policy aimed at citizens who use or abuse drugs. Measures included the creation of the Federal Bureau of Narcotics (FBN) in 1930 and the Narcotics Addict Rehabilitation Act of 1966, an institution and a policy that worked together to spur the War on Drugs and begin the steady uptick in incarceration rates that characterized the last third of the 20th century. In a well-orchestrated partnership with the media, the Federal Bureau of Narcotics produced an effective campaign of propaganda aimed at criminalizing and demonizing drug use in the United States. Harry Anslinger, who headed the agency from its inception until the early 1960s, was particularly outlandish in the myths he circulated regarding marijuana use and violent crime.

All of the data now available suggest that marijuana use does *not* induce users to violent or criminal behavior. Even during the FBN's propaganda heyday in the 1940s and 1950s, myths such as these about drugs were not believable to most Americans.[35] The government's overblown rhetoric on drugs and later the War on Drugs became the subject of humor, ridicule, and parody. Watching the 1930s propaganda film *Reefer Madness*, for example, has generated more amusement and cynicism than any sense of doom or danger for cannabis users. The film's suggestion that marijuana leads to violence, rape, and insanity was not believable 80 years ago, and it is not today.

Propaganda and Policy Formation

Believable or not, propaganda contributed to the cultural context out of which antidrug policy could take root during the Nixon years. In the 1960s and early 1970s, illegal drug use became a feature of the counterculture movements led by young people on college campuses and across the nation. In response, the federal government curtailed support for research into the health effects, social impact, and safety of controlled substances and illegal drugs.[36] President Nixon targeted drug addiction as a national public health issue at least partially in response to the glamorization of narcotics use that accompanied certain elements of the counterculture. Thus, in some way, Nixon's "law and order" edict—a political answer to progressive movements with respect to race, gender, and foreign policy—appealed to Middle American sentiments that demonized drug users in the same way that Southern segregationists demonized civil rights protesters. Law-and-order advocates called for peace in the streets and a return to an America unencumbered by the perils of drug use and addiction.

For the Nixon administration, drug abuse was "public enemy

number one."[37] This meant that the full resources of the federal government could be directed at the drug problem—especially criminal drug abusers. The establishment of the Special Action Office for Drug Abuse Prevention in 1971 signaled Nixon's push for policy acknowledgment of this particular issue. But the policies with the most irrevocable effects in the long term were not the ones aimed at treating addiction and abuse; they were the policies that relied on incarceration and an increasingly aggressive sensibility in the law enforcement community.

No Knocking Allowed

Nixon's War on Drugs implemented a policy of what is commonly referred to as the **no-knock warrant**. The Fourth Amendment to the Constitution protects U.S. citizens from unannounced and/or "unreasonable" searches by the government. The

police are not allowed to barge into your home whenever they want to; they must first obtain a warrant secured through a judicial process. In other words, they have to have approval from a judge in order to legally search a suspect's home. They also have to announce themselves and actually knock on your door before they enter your home. As one part of the War on Drugs, the Nixon administration declared it legal for law-enforcement officers to execute no-knock warrants, whereby police could forcibly enter your home without announcing themselves.

The no-knock policy was so regularly abused that it was repealed several years later. Nevertheless, over the four-decade history of the War on Drugs, a number of states have implemented laws or policies that effectively allow law enforcement to execute no-knock warrants—especially when the subject is suspected of being involved in drug trafficking. This is a special warrant issued by a judge that allows law-enforcement officers to enter a property without notifying residents.

Given the general resistance to changing the U.S. Constitution, the advent of the no-knock warrant marked a significant policy change brought on by the War on Drugs. Its implementation and re-implementation also underscore the role of aggressive police policy and tactics in fueling the mass incarceration that has accompanied the War on Drugs.

In general, law enforcement argues for the no-knock warrant in two situations: 1) Where the suspect is considered unusually dangerous. Thus, if law-enforcement officers were to knock on the door or announce themselves, the likelihood of violent armed confrontation with the suspect would increase exponentially; and 2) Where the suspect may have time to destroy evidence of their crimes before law enforcement can properly search their residence. While

both of these rationales seem straightforward, they leave room for broad interpretations and subjective understandings of any number of situations. For example, law-enforcement officers tend to think of drug dealers as unusually dangerous even though most of their engagements are with users and small-time dealers rather than high-level traffickers. Too many movies and TV shows have solidified the image of suspected criminals flushing drugs down the toilet for this not to be a common (if imagined) reason for the no-knock warrant. Yet destroying evidence in this way works only for small-time dealers or users, since large-scale traffickers typically have too much inventory to flush down the toilet at a moment's notice.

Securing no-knock warrants has become commonplace in the War on Drugs, while the judicial process does not appear to be functioning as a consistent bulwark of constitutional principles and civil rights. A 2000 study conducted by the *Denver Post* found that only about 8% of requests for no-knock warrants were rejected by judges over the course of one year in that city. In some cases, judges issued no-knock warrants without even being requested. This kind of aggressive police behavior, with the support of the judicial system, has eroded the tentative trust between law enforcement and the communities they are charged with protecting—especially poor communities of color where the War on Drugs raged most violently and persistently for decades.

In 1989, when the popular gangsta rap group NWA released the song "Fuck tha Police," many mainstream Americans were outraged without understanding how and why such anti-police sentiment had been fomented. The federal government responded by sending a warning letter from the FBI to the group. In 2015, the opening sequence of the film *Straight Outta Compton*, which chronicles NWA's rise to prominence and success, recounts the execution of a no-knock

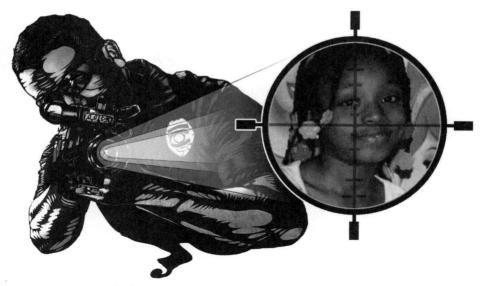

warrant at the home of an unsuspecting drug trafficker who employs Eazy-E, a member of the group. The images of a tank battering down a neighborhood home dramatizes the awesome force and social disruption that the no-knock policy allows in our communities. No one wants to live in a neighborhood infested with drugs or live next door to a crack house, but, given the military weapons at the disposal of local law enforcement and the legal leeway provided by policies produced on behalf of the war on drugs, it has become more and more clear how songs like "Fuck tha Police" became anthems in some communities.

In one notorious incident in 2010, police in Detroit conducted a no-knock raid on a residential home for a reality television show called *The First 48*, to be aired on the A&E cable network. In the process of executing (and videotaping) the raid, the officers killed a girl named Aiyanna Stanley-Jones while she lay sleeping on a couch in the living room. Aiyanna was just seven years old. The white officer responsible for the shooting was indicted and tried, but most of the charges were dismissed and the jury remained deadlocked on the charge of reckless use of a firearm; the judge declared a mistrial.

The tragic nature of this case, the age of the victim, and the sense too often that the lives of black people, poor people, and other people of color are simply disposable in the eyes of the criminal justice system, all helped to generate national attention around Aiyanna Stanley-Jones' death and the trial of the law officer in question. The movement for Black Lives, also known as the Black Lives Matter movement, has committed itself to monitoring these cases, organizing and protesting the institutions and policies that make these kinds of incidents occur too often in our society, and calling for the reformation and restructuring of law enforcement practices. In fact, many Americans might not know Aiyanna's name or the tragedy of her family and community if not for such movements and the protests triggered by such unfortunate cases. When an innocent seven-year old is shot in the head during a no-knock police raid, the consequences and "collateral damage" of the War on Drugs is cast in bold relief.

The American Civil Liberties Union (ACLU) in 2014 published extensive research on the efficacy of no-knock SWAT raids, focusing on more than 800 deployments by 20 different police departments. Although there was not enough *national* data to support definitive conclusions, the findings were instructive. First, 62% of the deployments were used in drug searches, and only about 25% of no-knock SWAT raids yielded contraband findings in targeted residences. The ACLU analysis did not find any instances of police being killed in raids, while, more often than not, civilians were injured and sometimes killed. While officers of the law no doubt have been injured and killed in SWAT raids, the data simply isn't sufficient to determine whether or not no-knock warrants help or hinder these cases.

Mandatory Minimum Sentencing

If the introduction of no-knock warrants set the stage for the irrevocable diminishment of constitutional rights in the home, the

policy of mandatory minimums— also introduced during the Nixon era—has made jail and/or prison the home of thousands for pre-set fixed sentences without any possibility of judicial consideration. The Attica prison uprising in September 1971 set the political stage for New York Governor Rockefeller to: 1) violently crush the rebellion, resulting in the deaths of 28 inmates and 10 guards; and 2) politicize the prisoner revolt, which was about the civil rights and humane treatment of prisoners, and 3) mark illegal drug use as the culprit for the behavior of the Attica insurgents as well as rampant criminality in the society at large. Governor Rockefeller believed that his state's criminal justice system was weak on crime and criminals, yielding a response that came to be known as the Rockefeller Drug

Laws. Among other things, the legislation implemented mandatory minimums for convicted drug criminals.

Mandatory minimums are fixed sentences ascribed to particular drug crimes, usually correlated with the possession of a specified amount of controlled substances and/or firearms. Their implementation, much like the legal impact of no-knock warrants, irrevocably altered American criminal justice. First, mandatory minimums increased rates of incarceration and the length of times being served. Once New York established itself as the toughest state on crime, many other states followed suit with mandatory minimum laws of their own.

Second, mandatory minimums eliminated the judge's role in determining sentences for a broad range of crimes associated with drug possession and/or drug trafficking. Without a judge's discretion as a central feature of the adjudication process, prosecutors assumed much more power and influence in the criminal justice process. The shift of power from "impartial" judges to biased prosecutors had awful consequences. Today, over 90% of criminal cases in the United States do not go to trial. The constitutional right to a trial by a jury of one's peers is nearly a myth—something much more likely to be seen on television or in a movie than in actual reality. More than 90% of cases end in plea bargaining between prosecutors armed with mandatory minimum sentences and defendants fearing an aggressive system with threats of long prison sentences. It's difficult to understand how a criminal justice system with a 90% plea rate is a fair and balanced, but the policy of mandatory minimum severed any connection between justice/fairness and the aggressive nature of the War on Drugs.

Reagan's War

The Watergate scandal led to President Nixon's resignation in August 1974, and the aftermath of those events raised hope that progressive forces in the world of American drug policy might mount a counter-initiative. President Jimmy Carter was a vocal advocate of decriminalizing marijuana as early as 1977, but a variety of geopolitical circumstances made him a one-term president. President Ronald Reagan, who took office in January 1981, quickly ushered in a new era of tough-on-crime, war-on-drugs policies. Indeed, it's been observed, Reagan's presidency

> marked the start of a long period of skyrocketing rates of incarceration, largely [due] to his unprecedented expansion of the drug war. The number of people [incarcerated] for nonviolent drug law offenses increased from 50,000 in 1980 to over 400,000 by 1997.[38]

Trends in American society made it seem prudent policy for President Reagan to continue and enhance the War on Drugs. With the

66

emergence of crack cocaine and with media-driven horror stories about addiction and criminality becoming part of the lore, the War on Drugs took on even greater urgency in the minds of American policy makers.

In October 1984, the U.S. Congress passed and President Reagan signed the landmark Comprehensive Crime Control Act. The first sweeping revision of the U.S. criminal code since the early 1900s, this legislation included new federal sentencing guidelines that directly and significantly expanded the Prison Industrial Complex. The guidelines signaled an ideological shift within the criminal justice system, particularly with respect to the purpose of prisons and the role that incarceration should play in modern society. The Sentencing Reform Act, which was part of the omnibus measure, marked the legislative death of any lingering belief in the American prison as a social institution where criminals could gain redemption or achieve rehabilitation through critical reflection. The new federal guidelines stipulated fixed minimum sentences for almost all federal crimes, and in doing so demonstrated that U.S. prison policy was focused more on punishing criminals than on rehabilitating them.

But it wasn't just policy makers and presidents who believed in the urgency of the War on Drugs or the dispensability of reform and rehabilitation as goals of incarceration for drug criminals. First Lady Nancy Reagan's "Just Say No" slogan and her public antidrug campaign have been repeatedly parodied and widely ridiculed for oversimplifying both the issue of drug abuse and the difficulty of overcoming addiction. During the 1980s, however, her campaign enjoyed wide support across the media and in the American public at large. Crack cocaine was seen as an unstoppable scourge. In the late 1980s, more than 60% of Americans believed that drug abuse was the number one problem in America. That figure made drug abuse and national perceptions of it in the 1980s one of the most prominent issues ever registered in the history of American public polling.[39]

PRISONER
POPULATION
GROWTH

With so much public and political support for the War on Drugs, finding the financial resources to fund the campaign was generally not an issue. In the 1980s and 1990s, however, a new financial incentive emerged that enhanced the aggressiveness of law enforcement departments in the conduct of the War on Drugs. **Asset forfeiture laws**—under which the property, money, or other material possessions of suspected drug criminals were forfeited to particular law-enforcement units engaged in an arrest if the goods or property had been acquired with illegal drug money—fundamentally altered the potential for judicial objectivity in prosecuting the drug wars. As James Kilgore wrote in *Understanding Mass Incarceration* (2015),

> [t]hroughout the country, police have seized real estate, personal property, and cash totaling fifteen billion, which they have legally pocketed to upgrade their operations and equipment.[40]

The potential for corruption in a system with notable biases is readily apparent in this kind of policy, but corruption is not even the most critical concern when considering how asset forfeiture feeds the War on Drugs and, in turn, the Prison Industrial Complex. If local and/or federal drug enforcement units are allowed to keep the "proceeds" from drug raids (if only for the department's benefit, rather than just an individual's benefit), does the policy offer any incentive that increases the likelihood of the war ever ending?

In the early 1990s, President Bill Clinton, who had campaigned on the promise of harm-reduction practices to help reverse the permanent drift of the War on Drugs, did little once in office to actually stop the campaign. In fact he continued to escalate the war and the policies that promoted

mass incarceration. One decision that mass-incarceration reformers today remember from the Clinton presidency is his rejection of a recommendation by the U.S. Sentencing Commission to address the sentencing disparities between crack and powder cocaine cases. Sentences for possession of crack cocaine were exponentially greater than sentences for powdered cocaine, even for much smaller amounts.

This particular aspect of drug policy was a consequence of mandatory minimums and the public hysteria generated by the crack epidemic of that era. Initially, however, it masked the racial underpinnings of these misguided policies. While crack isn't much more dangerous than powder cocaine, it is much cheaper to purchase and therefore found a stronger market in poorer inner-city communities of color. Because crack cocaine was relatively cheap and powder cocaine relatively expensive, the sentencing disparities around possession of these two types of the same drug also reflected racial disparities in drug laws, their enforcement, and punishment for violations. President Clinton's refusal to eliminate the disparity and ignore the commissions' recommendation was largely political—not wanting to be seen as weak on crime in the midst of a presidency frequently under the spotlight for its political vulnerabilities. The Barack Obama administration greatly reduced the disparity, but untold numbers of convicted drug offenders were still serving out sentences as a consequence of the unequitable sentencing policy.

President Obama proved generally more progressive in

addressing the policy challenges of the ongoing war on drugs and the Prison Industrial Complex. He became the first sitting president to visit a federal prison (touring Oklahoma's El Reno Federal Penitentiary in July 2015) and, in effect, the first president to attempt to humanize the American prisoner. Just prior to that visit, Obama delivered a speech on mass incarceration at the national convention of the NAACP that proved notable for a few reasons. For one thing, he actually used the term "mass incarceration." This may

seem like a low bar for such an urgent policy issue, but the standard had been set by the obstacle-ridden legislative environment within which the administration had to operate. Secondly, Obama clearly stated the opportunity costs of the Prison Industrial Complex and mass incarceration. For the $80 billion per year that we expend on mass incarceration, he pointed out, we could fund such vital initiatives such as pre-k education, free tuition at public universities, or doubling the salary of all public high-school teachers.

Situating the opportunity costs of mass incarceration within the context of public education makes both political and policymaking sense. PIC reformers and activists have clearly delineated the prison pipeline that, in too many cases, originates in our public school systems. Hearing a critique of mass incarceration from the executive office was considered important by those close to the issue, who hoped it would spur the political effort and critical policy changes needed to counter mass incarceration and the economic entrenchment of the PIC.

An End in Sight?

Obama's "mass incarceration speech" was also a call for criminal justice reform based on the rampant institutional bias in the system itself. He emphasized the costs and opportunity costs of mass incarceration, and the ways its economics make no sense. The way the president saw it, the fact that 2015 marked the first year that both mass incarceration and crime had declined nationally merely underscored the problems with what we (as a nation) pay to warehouse human beings for nonviolent drug offenses. The practical rationale for addressing this deeply racialized problem presented the very type of racial issue that America's first black president felt most comfortably addressing.

To appreciate the groundswell for criminal justice reform, it is important to recognize the broad range of initiatives, deeply troubling issues, and organized response of activist groups in the public arena. Black Lives Matter is wrestling directly with state-sanctioned murders of unarmed women and men of color. A variety of drug policy groups and law enforcement partners are calling for an end to the War on Drugs—perhaps America's greatest policy failure of the 20th century. And criminal justice advocates have radically challenged stop-and-frisk policies, racial profiling, sentencing disparities, and hiring practices throughout the country.

Together, the organizational energy of these groups and the attention they have brought to the issues are both sustainable and increasingly undeniable to politicians and policy makers. One can only hope that the hegemonic era of "law and order," without common sense, is coming to an end. President Obama's mass incarceration speech and his unprecedented visit to a federal prison suggest that criminal justice reform is both possible and practical.

Finally, it must be noted, even the end of the War on Drugs would not necessarily mean the end of mass incarceration in America. Nor would it finally demolish the partnerships of the Prison Industrial Complex. Of the 2.2 million Americans who are incarcerated, about 1.5 million are held at the federal and state levels, with the remaining 700,000 or so jailed in local facilities. Only about 20% of the inmates in state prisons and 50% of inmates in federal prisons are nonviolent drug offenders. Even if they were all released tomorrow, the United States would still lead the world in incarceration rates. But ending the war on drugs is vital. It would not bring an end to mass incarceration, but it would have a significant impact on the Prison Industrial Complex if we stopped aggressively incarcerating nonviolent (non-trafficking) drug users.

74

Chapter 4
Private Profits and Private Prisons

While only about 8% of prisons in the United States are privately held or privately controlled, the interface between private corporations and the Prison Industrial Complex is extensive. In order to fully appreciate the roles of private ownership and profiteering in the Prison Industrial Complex, it is essential to consider them in concert with each other and within the political rubric of neoliberalism.

Neoliberalism and Labor

Neoliberalism is a political ideology that informs and shapes economic and social policies that favor a free-market approach to policymaking. This includes, most importantly in the present context, the privatization of state-run businesses and social safety net institutions. Consider the public debate concerning the privatization of Social Security during the George W. Bush era, the corporate control of public charter schools, or the deregulation and corporate interventions in public utilities across the nation. Neoliberalism has driven bipartisan economic and social policy to a significant extent at least since the Reagan administration in the 1980s.

A by-product, perhaps even a central focus, of neoliberal policy initiatives at the federal level has been a systematic devaluation of the American worker. While some of this devaluation has been a function of regional trade policies such as NAFTA (North American  Free Trade Agreement), CAFTA (Central America Free Trade Agreement), and the proposed TPP (Trans-Pacific Partnership), the decline of labor unions and the labor movement in general has also been a factor in higher unemployment rates and rampant corporate outsourcing to cheaper labor markets abroad.[41] Some have argued that the underground illegal drug economy stepped into the economic space left by the dissolution of American manufacturing in the 1970s and the service industries in the 1990s.[42] The gaping holes in America's post-industrial economy of the late 1970s contributed to higher unemployment rates, which are generally consistent with higher crime rates. In effect, neoliberalism and its economic policies have contributed directly to the underground economies that underwrite the Prison Industrial Complex.

A Tangled Web

Since the days of convict leasing, American private industry has viewed the prison system as a viable opportunity for economic investment and exploitation—especially the potential for cheap, unregulated labor.[43] Corporations can participate in, and benefit from, the Prison Industrial Complex in multiple ways. They can create investment companies that partner with and/or financially support enterprises that use prison labor, or they can invest directly in private prison corporations, such as the Corrections Corporation of America (CCA) or The GEO Group. Some corporations use prison labor for both service jobs, such as call centers, and menial labor jobs, such as manufacturing plastic eating utensils. And a wide variety of companies do business with other companies that rely on prison labor or exploit inmates directly, such as phone service providers and minute-by-minute calling card vendors.

Given the variety of ways that many corporations benefit from inmate labor, the very notion of a private prison goes beyond the mere

terms of ownership and the flow of revenues. The depth and reach of corporate participation, reaping tremendous profits from human incarceration, makes the term "complex" entirely appropriate. In their book *The Prison Industrial Complex and the Global Economy* (2009), Eve Goldberg and Linda Evans cite the profiteering of giant telecom companies at the expense of inmates: "Communication companies like AT&T, Sprint and MCI are . . . gouging prisoners with exorbitant phone calling rates, often six times the normal long distance charge."[44]

Telecom service for the PIC generates about $1.2 billion annually. The level of profiteering provides additional incentives for corporations to continue to invest in the prison industry, even as the exploitation takes new and different shapes. In this case, exorbitant long-distance fees and other service charges create unsustainable debt for prisoners and cut them off from communicating with their families. That alienation contributes one more way to the dehumanization of prisoners and the compromise of basic human and civil rights in the PIC.

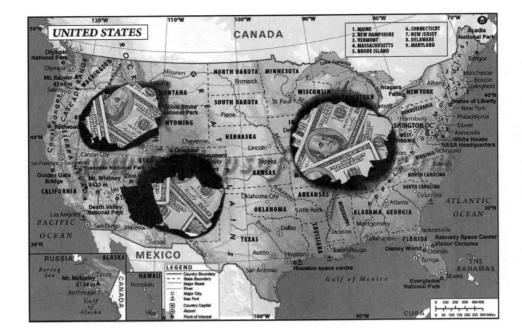

Human Capital

The human element in the profiteering of the Prison Industrial Complex expands in a variety ways (and means). Incarcerating people is costly, ranging from $25,000 to $60,000 annually per inmate.[45] Most of the funding comes from taxpayers. According to writer and activist James Kilgore, mass incarceration policies require committed, sustained spending for at least three "costly activities":

1) building prisons;

2) training and employing prison staff, and

3) equipping prisons and providing the various services prisoners require[46]

All of these costs and ongoing expenditures derive from the network of corporate interests that build and sustain prisons. Entire municipal economies are built on the prison industry. Some towns are lured into the industry with the promise of steady jobs and income levels that would not otherwise be possible in a post-industrial, neoliberal economy. While a number of towns in rural America enjoy prison-based economies, the demographics of the PIC reflect the geographic and economic consequences of the systemic warehousing of young black and brown folks in jails and prisons.

Casual conversations about the jobs and economic stability provided by the prison industry suggest a shallow understanding of the systemic challenges facing the United States. Struggling rural communities in the post-industrial era can hardly be blamed for considering their own economic viability and deciding that entering the prison economy makes sense for them. On the other hand, businesses, governments, and lobbyists that collude to make these options attractive to such communities should be held to a different level of accountability.

Industries That Profit from Prisons

Over the history of the PIC, many corporations and industries have directly and indirectly profited from mass incarceration in America. In a web posting titled "Identifying Businesses that Profit from Prison Labor," *Daily Kos* writer Bob Sloan catalogues numerous corporations with connections to the Prison Industrial

Complex in the several ways summarized above. (Many participate through a conservative political lobbying entity known as the American Legislative Exchange Council, or ALEC). The list provides a ready reference of longstanding, entrenched corporate interests in the PIC economy.

BANKS: *American General Financial Group, American Express Company, Bank of America, Community Financial Services Corporation, Credit Card Coalition, Credit Union National Association, Inc., Fidelity Investments, Harris Trust & Savings Bank, Household International, LaSalle National Bank, J.P. Morgan & Company, Non-Bank Funds Transmitters Group*

ENERGY PRODUCERS/OIL: *American Petroleum Institute, Amoco Corporation, ARCO, BP America, Inc., Caltex Petroleum, Chevron Corporation, ExxonMobil Corporation, Mobil Oil Corporation, Phillips Petroleum Company.*

ENERGY PRODUCERS/UTILITIES: *American Electric Power Association, American Gas Association, Center for Energy and Economic Development, Commonwealth Edison Company, Consolidated Edison Company of New York, Inc., Edison Electric Institute, Independent Power Producers of New York, Koch Industries, Inc., Mid-American Energy Company, Natural Gas Supply Association, PG&E Corporation/ PG&E National Energy Group, U.S. Generating Company.*

81

INSURANCE: *Alliance of American Insurers, Allstate Insurance Company, American Council of Life Insurance, American Insurance Association, Blue Cross and Blue Shield Corporation, Coalition for Asbestos Justice, (This organization was formed in October 2000 to explore new judicial approaches to asbestos litigation." Its members include ACE-USA, Chubb & Son, CNA service mark companies, Fireman's Fund Insurance Company, Hartford Financial Services Group, Inc., Kemper Insurance Companies, Liberty Mutual Insurance Group, and St. Paul Fire and Marine Insurance Company. Counsel to the coalition is Victor E. Schwartz of the law firm of Crowell & Moring in Washington, D.C., a longtime ALEC ally.) Fortis Health, GEICO, Golden Rule Insurance Company, Guarantee Trust Life Insurance, MEGA Life and Health Insurance Company, National Association of Independent Insurers, Nationwide Insurance/National Financial, State Farm Insurance Companies, Wausau Insurance Companies, Zurich Insurance.*

PHARMACEUTICALS: *Abbott Laboratories, Aventis Pharmaceuticals, Inc., Bayer Corporation, Eli Lilly & Company, GlaxoSmithKline, Glaxo Wellcome, Inc., Hoffman-LaRoche, Inc., Merck & Company, Inc., Pfizer, Inc., Pharmaceutical Research and Manufacturers of America (PhRMA), Pharmacia Corporation, Rhone-Poulenc Rorer, Inc., Schering-Plough Corporation, Smith, Kline & French, WYETH, a division of American Home Products Corporation.*

82

MANUFACTURING: *American Plastics Council, Archer Daniels Midland Corporation, AutoZone, Inc. (aftermarket automotive parts), Cargill, Inc., Caterpillar, Inc., Chlorine Chemistry Council, Deere & Company, Fruit of the Loom, Grocery Manufacturers of America, Inland Steel Industries, Inc., International Game Technology, International Paper, Johnson & Johnson, Keystone Automotive Industries, Motorola, Inc., Procter & Gamble, Sara Lee Corporation.*

TELECOMMUNICATIONS: *AT&T, Ameritech, BellSouth Telecommunications, Inc., GTE Corporation, MCI, National Cable and Telecommunications Association, SBC Communications, Inc., Sprint, UST Public Affairs, Inc., Verizon Communications, Inc.*

TRANSPORTATION: *Air Transport Association of America, American Trucking Association, The Boeing Company, United Airlines, United Parcel Service (UPS).*

OTHER U.S. COMPANIES: *Amway Corporation, Cabot Sedgewick, Cendant Corporation, Corrections Corporation of America, Dresser Industries, Federated Department Stores, International Gold Corporation, Mary Kay Cosmetics, Microsoft Corporation, Newmont Mining Corporation, Quaker Oats, Sears, Roebuck & Company, Service Corporation International, Taxpayers Network, Inc., Turner Construction, Wal-Mart Stores, Inc.*[47]

Prisons are Private Too

In addition to BIG business networks and the powerful corporate interface with the PIC, there are also private prisons per se. These are corporate-owned and -operated facilities that have taken advantage of neoliberal ideas about the role that private corporations can play in managing and providing public services.

83

Private prisons emerged and developed their business models for the original purpose of immigrant incarceration. In 1983, CCA won a government contract to own and operate the first private prison in the United States; it was an immigrant detention center.[48] Today, private corporations house almost half of all immigrants detained by the United States.

In the years that followed, CCA extended its reach in the private-prison industry and continued to do so for the next several decades. Along with The GEO Group, formerly known as Wackenhut Corrections Corporation, the two companies remain the largest for-profit prison enterprises in the United States today. Both companies have publicly traded stock, and both profit directly from incarcerating people.

The particular moral (and social) dilemma of the for-profit prison industry is worth noting again. Private corporations—especially but not exclusively CCA and GEO Group—are not necessarily beholden to the American judicial system or policy ideals. When they establish corporate goals, make financial decisions, and manage shareholder

expectations, they need not take into account the social concerns of the community or the criminal justice system—i.e., whether or not prison facilities serve the long-term public good. They do not have to think about rehabilitating (or punishing) prisoners; nor are they accountable to any kind of parole process or sensible estimates regarding recidivism (the rate at which released prisoners return to prison after committing additional crimes). The only things that CCA, GEO Group, and other such firms have to consider is how to build prisons efficiently, how to manage prisons efficiently, and ultimately

how to keep their prisons at full capacity, earn a profit, and build more prisons.

According to one source, corporations such as CCA and GEO have donated more than $10 million to political candidates and spent more than $25 million on various lobbying initiatives since 1989.[49] For-profit prison companies tend to support candidates who support legislation that supports the PIC in any way—like Arizona's 2010 anti-immigration bill (S.B. 1070) or California's notorious Three Strikes Law in 1994. By doing so, they help to elect and reelect politicians who push policies that fill American jails with immigrants and nonviolent criminals.

The economic results of these efforts have been fantastic for both corporations and the private-prison industry in general. Between 1990 and 2009, as the inmate population of private prisons increased 1600 percent (outpacing the rate of increase in public prisons at the very height of the PIC's expansion)[50], CCA and GEO Group together generated over $3 billion per year.

Despite its strong profitability, the private prison industry claims to operate efficiently and save the government money. None of these claims have been verified via independent research or studies conducted by neutral parties, however, and indeed there is evidence to the contrary. In 2012, the American Friends Service Committee (AFSC) published a report, titled "Private Prisons: The Public's Problem," based on a review of the Arizona prison system. (The examination was as comprehensive as possible given the limitations on data collection by private corporations whose interests are not served by participating in such studies.) The results were less than favorable:

> *The data shows that private prisons under contract with the state cost more than equivalent units operated by the state Department of Corrections. AFSC estimates that in 2009 and 2010, Arizona overpaid for these units by as much as $7 million. If the state adds 2,000 medium-security private beds, as it has proposed, Arizonans could be losing over $10 million every year on private prisons.*[51]

The Government Accountability Office (GAO), an investigative arm of Congress, has also conducted studies that compare public versus private facilities in a number of states, including Texas, California, and Tennessee. Investigators encountered a number of challenges in collecting accurate data—reflecting the private sector's resistance to government oversight in neoliberal times—

and the results have been mixed. Not adequately accounted for are some of the nuanced differences between private and public prisons. Public prisons, for example, tend to house more dangerous criminals than private prisons. Their greater security needs thus require more resources, better equipment and facilities, and more highly trained staff and employees. Moreover, public prisons cannot cut some of the costs that private prisons can due to public standards, fixed allocations, and the limitations of the PIC infrastructure.

In Great Britain, where private firms operate penal institutions that house 18 percent of the nation's prisoners (higher than in the United States), privatization has been ridiculed as an abject failure. In 2015, some 25 years into the private prison "experiment," British government statistics revealed higher rates of violent fighting, drug usage, hunger strikes, inmate escapes, rape/sexual assault, and suicide/self-harm than in public prison counterparts.[52]

If the studies from across the pond are not compelling enough to underscore the challenges in the private prison industry, then the United States need look no farther than the all-too-public mishaps of the private PIC over the years. In July 2010, three inmates escaped from an Arizona prison operated by the Management and Training Company (MTC). One of the escapees, John McCluskey, was then

linked to a double-murder in New Mexico. A follow-up investigation by state authorities revealed gross oversights in security at the MTC facility, suggesting that the escape and resulting murders had been avoidable.

Perhaps the most notorious example of the inadequacies of private prisons was a 1999 scandal at the Northeast Ohio Correctional Facility in Youngstown, owned and operated by CCA. In just over a year of operation, the facility witnessed six escapes, more than a dozen stabbings, and seven murders. Amazingly, CCA decided to close the prison *not* because of its failures to protect inmates and the surrounding public, but because the facility ceased to be profitable.[53]

These are just two of many examples of egregious security and safety issues in private prisons. No doubt there have been others, never revealed. At both the state and federal level, private prisons resist use of the Freedom of Information Act to uncover their problems, a luxury not afforded to government-run institutions of incarceration.

The 2010 annual report of the CCA, meanwhile, contained the following statement:

> *The demand for our facilities and services could be adversely affected by the relaxation of enforcement efforts, leniency in conviction or parole standards and sentencing practices*

or through the decriminalization of certain activities that are currently proscribed by our criminal laws. For instance, any changes with respect to drugs and controlled substances or illegal immigration could affect the number of persons arrested, convicted, and sentenced, thereby potentially reducing demand for correctional facilities to house them.

The statement suggests much about the social, political, and economic issues at the crux of the private prison industry and its role in the PIC. To begin with, framing the report in the language of supply and demand limits the company's accountability in the social sphere and underscores the fact that private corporate interests need not be concerned with anything other than their own bottom line. Given the national conversations regarding aggressive law enforcement, the decriminalization of controlled substances, and racial bias in the criminal justice system, the CCA statement smacks of a profound disconnect between its corporate interests and public discourses directly related to the industry within which they are trying to protect "demand."

The national conversation on criminal justice has come to focus on police brutality, implicit racial bias, and the various tactics that

drive and underwrite mass incarceration policy. Conversations about "stop and frisk," for example, have shifted in response to the issues raised by racial bias in where, how, and on whom the tactic is used.

Broken Windows

Perhaps unbeknownst to CCA, the activities of municipal law enforcement have prompted a skeptical rethinking of the entire approach to criminal justice in America, driven by young protesters on behalf of the movement for Black Lives (BLM). Police tactics like stop and frisk, racial profiling, and other aggressive measures are considered part of a broader strategy of law enforcement—and the social theories behind it—referred to as "broken windows" policing. Emerging from the War on Drugs of the 1980s, the general theory was first defined in an article by George Kelling and James

Q. Wilson in *The Atlantic* titled "Broken Windows: The Police and Neighborhood Safety" (March 1982). The basic idea was to police minor crimes, such as loitering and disorderly conduct, as a means of reducing major crimes in the longer term. The underlying theory was that a community with fewer "broken windows"—neighborhood disruption and disorder—will ultimately have less serious violent crime.

Whether or not this policing strategy accounted for the precipitous decline in violent crime experienced across the United States is difficult to prove. Some social scientists attribute the decrease in serious crime to better access to reproductive rights for poor families. We simply cannot prove that broken windows policing works the way criminologists and law enforcement officials say it does.

Here's what we do know: in the hearts and minds of law enforcement, people of color—especially young Black men—are themselves considered the broken windows. Their mere presence in certain environments—on a street corner, outside a convenience store, behind the wheel of a car—compels the police to take action, sometimes with excessive force. Too often the policing of "broken windows" is itself a broken policy that continues to break the trust between the community and law enforcement. And it certainly leads to higher incarceration rates. The idea that corporations can set an agenda so crucial to the public yet so counter to some of the most vital discourses in our nation underscores the challenges inherent in privatization movements where "efficiency" and profit trump the public trust.

The Real Problem

Immediately eradicating private prisons would not dismantle the PIC completely, but it would be a good start. In a 2105 article titled "The Real Problem With Private Prisons," criminal justice advocate Eric Lotke suggests that the central issue with private prisons is that they exist at all.[54] The "real" issue with private prisons, as he puts it, boils down to availability. In order for prisons to be authorized and built by traditional processes with public resources, the government of the municipality or state must ultimately have the votes or the will of the people to do so. Since the War on Drugs, however, public prisons have exceeded their capacity. When that happens, private prisons offer an expedient for governments that choose to circumvent their own bureaucratic processes—the very processes that should take into account the communities and constituencies they serve. Sadly, the Prison Industrial Complex has been able to thrive in environments where privatization overdetermines and undermines the public interest.

Chapter 5

Youth, Immigration, and Solitary Confinement

Thankfully, mass incarceration emerged as a high-profile issue in our national conversation during the 2015-2016 presidential nominating season. The discussion took place among the candidates pursuing the Democratic nomination more so than those seeking the Republican nod, but the fact that mass incarceration was mentioned at all—and identified as a wrongheaded policy—was an important marker of progress in the ongoing struggle to upend the Prison Industrial Complex. Perhaps we are entering an era in which the "tough on crime" mandate across the two-party system is waning. And if that is happening, we can begin to imagine a future in which the PIC is dismantled. We can certainly hope that this is the case and demand that our political leaders take notice of the data that expose the problems in our criminal justice system.

Superpredators/Super Bias

In February 2016, a Black Lives Matter (BLM) activist named Ashley Williams disrupted a $500/person fundraising event being hosted by the Hillary Clinton campaign. All Williams did to make her point was hold up a sign with words from a speech given by then First Lady Hillary Clinton in 1996, during the reelection campaign for her husband, President Bill Clinton. "We have to bring them to heel," the sign read.

Hillary's speech had come two years after the signing of President Bill Clinton's infamous 1994 Crime Bill, or the Violent Crime Control and Law Enforcement Act. The most sweeping federal crime legislation in U.S. history, his initiative directly fed the monster that the PIC was already on its way to becoming. In support of those policies and her husband's candidacy for reelection, the First Lady referred to certain American youth gangs as "superpredators" and suggested, "[w]e can talk about why they ended up that way, but first we have to bring them to heel."

The historical context of the quote is important to remember. It was the mid-1990s, and the national perception of crime and crime rates had not caught up with data clearly showing a *decline* in violent crime—even among urban youth associated with gang culture. But facts about crime don't always matter as much as *perceptions* of crime do; nor do the facts always matter in a presidential campaign. In short, First Lady Clinton was playing into a well-worn script in American politics—that being

tough on crime was essential for political leaders to earn the trust of the electorate. Despite evidence to the contrary, the American mainstream harbored irrational fears of an imminent future in which nihilistic young predators—inevitably young Black men—would control urban communities through violence and drug dealing. Hillary Clinton's speech that day was designed to shore up President Bill Clinton's bona fides as a tough-on-crime Democrat poised to bring animalistic predators "to heel."

The fact that Ashley Williams and the Black Lives Matter movement would seize upon this language ten years later, and use it to push presidential candidates to wrestle with the problems of the Prison Industrial Complex, is perhaps as significant as the context in which the comments were originally made. While some of the national news media did not cover the disruption, and others tried to explain away Williams' sign based on the critical context of the moment, activists engaged in revealing the problems of the American criminal justice system were fully aware of the role that language plays in supporting the policies that exact justice unequally in terms of race, class, and gender.

The First Lady's comments still rankled. Her refusal to understand or discuss why young people turn to crime in the first place remained a telling reflection of the problematic ways in which crime policy too often is made. In the absence of real information about eroding public schools, the outsourcing of manufacturing

and service jobs, the impact of regional trade agreements on the American worker, and a host of other factors, the notion that hordes of young people are predisposed to committing violent crimes reinforces the shallow thinking that some young people—young *Black* people—are just naturally criminal. Without any recognition of social and economic context, the notion that "We can talk about these things if we want to but . . ." simply suggests that the only way to address the problem is through punishment and incarceration.

In some ways, the dismissal of (or failure to understand) the facts is more damning than the dehumanizing language of the statement itself. It reduces policy formation to reactionary platitudes that ignore the structural realities that cultivate and produce certain behaviors. No one—not then and not now—can argue with the fact that concentrated poverty and high crime rates go hand in hand. Not acknowledging that fact honestly and upfront is a disingenuous play into people's fears about crime in society.

Obviously it does not address the social problems associated with criminality and the PIC in a civilized, humane way to think of bringing young people "to heel." The phrase typically refers to the discipline, training, and control of animals, not human beings. Dogs and horses are "brought to heel." BLM activists understand that this is precisely the type of language that facilitates the inhumane treatment of the incarcerated—especially young people. Moreover, the thinking that underlies this kind of language is a direct reflection of the racial biases that contaminate the entire system and have done so since the earliest iterations of the American prison system.

Clinton was not speaking off the cuff. She took the term "superpredator" from a political scientist who became nationally recognized in the 1990s for his theory of juvenile violent crime. The scholar, named John DiIulio, distanced himself from his own research in 2001, just as he was appointed to direct the George W. Bush White House Office of Faith-Based and Community Initiatives.

In the meantime, DiIulio argued that a combination of demographic shifts in the population (i.e., a surge in Black male youth) and the socialization of many of these youths by older, more violent Black people in their neighborhoods was, in effect, producing what he called "a new generation of street criminals—the youngest, biggest and baddest generation any society has ever known."[55]

The vision of a future dominated by marauding superpredators soon took hold in the American political imagination, with terrifying political consequences. Support for tough-on-crime policies continued unabated. Funding for the War on Drugs and the outsourcing of private prisons likewise continued to thrive into the next decade. Whether or not political leaders and policymakers are willing to admit it, once again the claims of an academic— purportedly supported by sound research—set in motion a series of policy recommendations, laws, and practices that put an inordinate, inequitable number of poor people of color into the Prison Industrial Complex. Fear and prejudice prevailed.

This superpredator theory was, in the end, soundly debunked. The juvenile crime rate dropped by more than half over the period that DiIulio predicted it would skyrocket. In the meantime, however, the popularity of the concept was one of several factors that facilitated a national movement to try youthful offenders as adults for violent crimes. Legislators heeded the call. Between 1992 and 1999, 49 states and the District of Columbia made it easier to try juveniles as adults.

Some states removed consideration of youth altogether, replacing discretion with compulsory triggers. By 2012, there were 28 states across the nation that were handing out mandatory life-without-parole sentences to juveniles.[56]

Nowhere was this theory adopted into policy more pervasively than in the states of Pennsylvania and Louisiana. Pennsylvania, according to information collected in 2015 by the Phillips Black Project, a nonprofit law organization, had the most prisoners serving juvenile life sentences—376. Louisiana followed closely behind with 247, representing the highest per-capita rate in the nation. Nearly 200 of the 247 juvenile life sentences in Louisiana were given to African Americans.

The superpredator theory has remained stuck in the collective consciousness of the American criminal justice system. Only recently, in 2012 and 2016, has the U.S. Supreme Court ruled in favor of juvenile humanity and the possibility of rehabilitation by banning life-without-parole sentences for juveniles. Still, young people of color—especially the poor—have continued to be vulnerable to the policies that power the PIC. In the end, it comes to down to one simple fact: It is easiest to demonize those who don't yet vote and who, because of our criminal justice policies, may never get the chance.

Perhaps the best way to sum up the pervasive consensus for this kind of PIC rhetoric and practice in American politics is that Clinton's rival for the Democratic nomination in 2016—the "democratic Socialist" Bernie Sanders—voted for the crime bill in 1994 and, like Hillary and Bill Clinton, came to regret his support.

Anti-Family Immigration Policy

Another realm of federal policy that tends to have a disparate impact on young people is immigration. Like the superpredator theory and its legislative consequences, American immigration policy in the late 20th and early 21st centuries relies more on fear and racism than it does on the actual facts of immigration.

In the 2010s, net immigration into the United States has been close to zero; and there has been *no* net immigration from Mexico. Yet the rhetoric of building walls and deporting "illegals" continues to be the order of the day in the national discourses on immigration policy. From the nation's earliest immigration policies through the 1980s, crossing the U.S. border illegally was considered a minor civil offense. In the 1990s, however, shadows of the Prison Industrial Complex began creeping into ideas about immigration. The policies that followed contributed significantly both to the prison population and to the role of private corporations in the American penal system.

Without any evidence that increased penalties would reduce unauthorized entry into the United States, federal policy makers in the mid-1990s made illegal border crossing a criminal

offense. Prosecutions for illegally crossing the border rose from less than 4,000 annually at the beginning of the Clinton administration to more than 31,000 per year during the George W. Bush administration, skyrocketing to 91,000 in 2013 under President Barack Obama.[57] The rush of new prosecutions contributed in no small measure to the expansion of the Prison Industrial Complex into its grotesque current form and has had a direct impact on the lives and families of undocumented youth.

Most immigrant families, documented or not, enter the United States for work-related reasons. Many of those who enter the country for economic advantage are lured by the promise of jobs with large corporations that deliberately circumvent labor law and hiring practices. Once again, the facts of the situation are often left out of the discourse. And so, true to form for the Prison Industrial Complex, the policies that made the criminal justice system more aggressive toward immigrant communities of color was soon producing conviction rates that outstripped the capacity of federal prisons and detention centers to accommodate the influx of newly minted convicts. The Federal Bureau of Prisons responded by outsourcing the problem to private corporations. Today, the Corrections Corporation of America (CCA) and The GEO Group (formerly Wackenhut) own and operate nine of the 11 private detention centers where the population of convicted undocumented immigrants is housed.

The Bureau of Prisons thus relies on private corporations to manage a problem of the government's own policymaking. The government spends in excess of $600 million annually to outsource the consequences of a broken federal immigration policy to private corporations with a track record of cutting corners rather than cutting costs. One of the recurring problems in the immigrant-only private prison system is an abysmal record on health care for inmates. Reporters and activists have uncovered incidents and conditions best described as atrocities that are endemic to the privatized sector of the PIC. While politicians make hay over the need for walls, the lack of humane levels of health care has been left out of the debate about the nation's immigration policy. And, as in the case of most of unforeseen consequences of the PIC, it is children who suffer most from the deficiency.

Solitary Confinement, Solitary Death

Like our broken immigration policy and the political rhetoric of toughness on crime, another aspect of the PIC with a disparate impact on American youth is the tortuous practice of solitary confinement. Solitary confinement is the practice of incarcerating inmates in a small cell for up to 24 hours per day, with limited or no contact with other human beings. It bars family and conjugal visits, reading materials, educational programming, and medical treatment. Prisoners forced into solitary confinement are often physically abused, tortured, or mistreated in other ways. Some are subjected to sensory deprivation, various forms of restraint or physical confinement, and the periodic use of stun guns and stun grenades.[58]

Like most of the worst aspects of the Prison Industrial Complex, the widespread use of solitary confinement began in the 1970s and continued to expand through the "heyday" of the PIC from 1985 to 1994. Today, the American prison population includes more than 80,000 inmates in solitary confinement.

A number of side effects, both physical and mental, are derived from ongoing isolation and physical punishment over the course of days, months, and sometimes years. Among the psychological consequences are paranoia, hallucinations, post-traumatic stress disorder, and suicidal inclinations.[59] Most of the mental effects have a greater impact on young inmates because their brains are still developing and because of their youthful vulnerability.

In certain systems and in some regions of the country, officials of the PIC acknowledge the inhumane treatment endemic to all

forms of solitary confinement. Some of this recognition came to the state of New York after the tragic case of Kalief Browder. In 2010, at the age of 16, Browder was arrested for allegedly stealing a backpack. Charged with second-degree robbery, he refused to plea bargain and was unable to make bail. As a result, he was incarcerated for three years without ever being convicted of a crime. Held at the Rikers Island Prison Complex in New York City, a group of jails notorious for their draconian conditions, Browder spent two thirds of his time there in solitary confinement. It was

later reported that Rikers guards starved him as punishment for repeated suicide attempts. Videotapes showed officers and other inmates pummeling and kicking him.

As brought to light by journalist Jennifer Gonnerman in the pages of *The New Yorker* magazine, Browder's plight dramatized the devastating long-term effects of solitary confinement and became a symbol of the broken criminal justice system. Released in May 2013, Browder tried to get his life back on track but never fully recovered from his prison experiences. In June 2015, he committed suicide by hanging himself at his parents' home.

Kalief Browder remains a living symbol of the ways our Prison Industrial Complex treats young people and the brutality of solitary confinement. That a teenager could be confined for three years—most of them in solitary—without even being convicted of a crime begins to tell us how broken the system is, to demonstrate the inordinate backlog of cases in a criminal justice system the size of New York's, and to underscore the inherent bias in bail levels for poor and working-class citizens. While Browder's story drew national attention and put pressure on political leaders to initiate change, his experiences should serve as an ongoing reminder of just how horrific the Prison Industrial Complex can be to our children.

Chapter 6
Recidivism and Real Reform

The rates of recidivism for the Prison Industrial Complex reveal at least one unfortunate fact: American incarceration is no longer invested in rehabilitation. Recidivism—defined as the rate at which released prisoners return to prison, or the percentage of released prisoners that return to prison—represents a powerful referendum on why the PIC must be abolished and an important rationale for why the policies that shape and inform mass incarceration must be eradicated.

The End of the Rehab Myth

A 2014 study conducted by the U.S. Department of Justice found that two thirds of individuals released from U.S. prisons in 2005 were rearrested within three years; three fourths were rearrested within five years.[60] If the majority of those who are imprisoned end up back in prison within five years, then perhaps the PIC should be recognized as a system that benefits from and promotes the warehousing of human bodies and that, in many cases, the facilities of incarceration are actually preparing prisoners for more criminal activity and an ongoing life of confinement and/or enslavement.

As discussed in earlier chapters, the origins of the American penitentiary—both in name and in social and institutional structuring—suggest that jails and prisons should serve as spaces of reflection for members of society who may have lost their way. Legal scholars and the social architects of the early United States believed in the possibility of redemption through silent reflection, labor, and isolation. It was not until well into the 20th century, with the advent of "law and order" ideology as a fixture of American politics and the growing sentiment that criminal behavior is irredeemable, that the social context for rampant recidivism began to be established. Robert Martinson's infamous 1974 article "What Works" actually suggested that *nothing* works in terms of rehabilitating prisoners. His impact on public policy and the public's perception of crime and the limits (or impossibility) of rehabilitation was profound and long-lasting. Indeed it could be argued that Martinson's work, in tandem with President Nixon's initiation of the War on Drugs, laid the ideological foundations for recidivism in the PIC—especially for drug offenders.

We can understand this unfortunate set of circumstances through the eyes of professionals on all sides of the legal process. In his book *Let's Get Free* (2009), former criminal prosecutor Paul

Butler takes a searing look back at the profession of which he was once a part. His experiences as a prosecutor made him skeptical about the viability of prosecuting crimes that are socially perpetual, like prostitution and drug possession. Butler paints a picture of prosecution lawyers as being game-oriented, focused on winning by any means necessary. In his view, the overly aggressive nature of modern-day criminal prosecutions, the outrageously high plea rate, and the racial and class biases in the system all add up to one thing: The U.S. criminal justice system practices "legal hate."

High recidivism rates reflect the legalized hate practices of the PIC—solitary   confinement, forced labor, rape, and gang violence. There's no mistaking the truth. Conditions within prisons directly contribute to the high rates of return. Moreover, according to some studies, more than half of all recidivists are charged with more serious crimes than their initial cause of entry into the PIC. This intimates an awful possibility: that the PIC is not rehabilitating criminals, but it is training them to become even more hardened and more violent criminals. Intended or not, recidivism feeds the PIC and simultaneously reveals its most critical secret: the PIC feeds off of itself.

It is somewhat ironic that we rely on the U.S. Department of Justice (DOJ) for so much critical information on the Prison Industrial Complex. In this case, the data on recidivism is key to

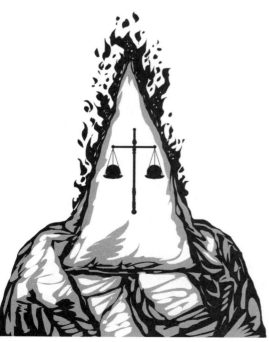

our understanding of the failures of the PIC and our withering social investment in the possibility of rehabilitation. In assessing these and other figures, it is important to remember the DOJ's role in the PIC has not always been constructive or objective. In the early 1990s, the department deliberately exaggerated the threat of violent crime in America, making an artificial case for more incarceration.[61] And to make a case for the construction of more prisons, the DOJ cited a

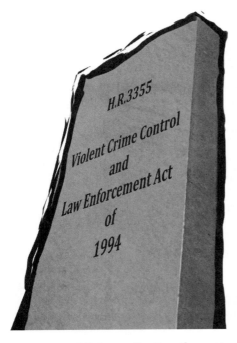

1987 government study indicating that incarcerating just one prisoner saved society more than $400,000 per year. If this sounds too good to be true, that's because it is not true. The "study" in question was based on the fantastic claim that an alleged criminal left un-incarcerated would commit over 180 street crimes per year, at a cost of about $2000 per crime. The researchers eventually retracted their claims, but the damage may have already been done. The early 1990s brought the rapid expansion of the PIC, with the initial data on recidivism reflecting the nation's belief that locking up criminals was the only way to lower crimes rates.[62]

Inside Education

The entire history of the PIC has seen repeated, marked dissonance between research, research accuracy, and the policies of mass incarceration. One critical issue directly related to recidivism rates is that of education in prisons. Among the measures included in President Bill Clinton's 1994 Crime Bill—epitomizing and institutionalizing the "tough on crime," law-and-order politics of the time—was the elimination of Pell Grants for federal prisoners. Pell Grant funding provided support for prisoners to take college courses. Individual states followed suit, and by 1995 only about 2% of college programs in American prisons were still in place.[63]

It hardly takes a government report or academic study to understand that educating prisoners can expand their options and improve their quality of life after release. But public sentiment toward criminals and prisoners during the 1990s was shaped completely by the law- and-order ideology that had triggered the War on Drugs. For too many Americans, providing educational support to incarcerated criminals was inconsistent with the principles of punishment and confinement. The Crime Bill of 1994 certainly seems archaic and inhumane in hindsight, as it exacerbated the worst aspects of the PIC by expanding privatization and diminishing the last vestiges of the possibility of rehabilitation. Yet the legislation was well-received by politicians and the public at the time, even though the inherent racial and class biases of the PIC were readily apparent.

Studies do indicate, of course, that education and access to education in prison reduce recidivism and produce more favorable reentry outcomes for former prisoners trying to make (or remake) a life outside the PIC. According to an Urban Institute study in the early 2000s, participants in vocational and educational programs in prison were, upon release, more employable, employed for longer periods of time, and committed fewer crimes than their counterparts who did not take part in such programs.[64] There is little question that education in prison reduces recidivism rates and limits the PIC's cyclical processes of incarceration.

The Cost of No Reentry

Since the early 2000s, public sentiment in the United States has started to shift with respect to the PIC. In addition, the exorbitant costs of the PIC in both human and monetary capital have forced many states to adopt more humane and economically sensible policies to address the problems of mass incarceration. Contemporary studies have contributed to a mounting body of data once again suggesting that programs within the prison system might help reduce recidivism. Many of the same studies also suggest that alternatives to incarceration might be more effective at rehabilitating nonviolent offenders—but that could be the subject of another entire book.

In 2008, the U.S. Congress passed the Second Chance Act (SCA), which supports state, local, and tribal governments and nonprofit organizations in their efforts to reduce recidivism and improve outcomes for people returning from state and federal prisons, local jails, and juvenile facilities. "Passed with bipartisan support and signed into law by President George W. Bush on April 9, 2008, the legislation authorized federal grants for vital programs and systems reform aimed at improving the reentry process."[65]

Parole and Probation Under Reagan

The focus on reducing recidivism and providing more robust support for reentry programs are the cornerstones of what, by some accounts, is a fairly anemic prison reform program proffered at the federal and state levels. With respect to recidivism, a few final points are worth exploring here briefly.

For the most part, when people think about recidivism rates in the PIC, the general assumption is that re-incarceration is driven largely by criminals just being criminals—that they continue to commit crimes after being released because they are naturally and irreversibly criminal. Upon closer investigation of the PIC, however, one finds other factors within the system itself that drive recidivism rates.

Prior to the Reagan administration in the 1980s, there was still a small modicum of hope for rehabilitation and redemption in the PIC. But once President Reagan doubled down on the War on Drugs and once the ideology of law and order was invigorated with new rhetoric and policy initiatives, the shift to a purely punishment-driven PIC was cemented. The transition was clearly reflected in changes to the approach to parole and probation. Under the rehabilitation ethic of the penitentiary system, and throughout the early history of parole and probation in America, parole and/or probation officers were committed to keeping their clients *out* of jail. Believe it or not,

mandatory drug testing was not an original feature of probation. But the law-and-order crowd sincerely believed that parole boards were too lenient and that too many "hardened criminals" were not serving long enough sentences.

Reagan's War on Drugs changed the fundamental approaches to both the parole and probationary processes. In the 1980s, law enforcement institutions enhanced the role of what was referred to as "technical violations," making it easier to re-incarcerate paroled prisoners and those on probation for various offenses. Technical violations are exactly what they sound like—violations of a rule or regulation that should be considered technical or petty depending upon perspective. In the present context,

> [t]echnical violations can include missing a scheduled meeting with a parole officer, failing to tell the parole officer of a change in employment or residence, failing to disclose parole status to an employer or landlord, being out of your county without permission, and(or) getting a positive drug test.[66]

Under the new approach, a positive drug test even for a former prisoner previously convicted of a drug-related offense might still constitute grounds for re-incarceration in some parole cases. In effect, parole and probation tactics during the 1980s became much more aggressive, contributing to mass incarceration rather than serving the original purposes of facilitating rehabilitation and reentry into society.

As of 1980, only about 17% of prisoners in the United States were serving time for parole violations. By the end of the 1990s, fully one third of prisoners had been re-incarcerated for parole violations; two-thirds of those had been re-incarcerated for technical violations.[67]

Of the many failures of the PIC briefly catalogued in this book, the shift in the administration of parole and probation ranks as one of the most profound. It underscores yet again the abandonment of rehabilitation as a guiding principle of the criminal justice system, and it highlights the incapacity of the system to act fairly and to treat humans with patience and dignity. This is especially devastating given the inherent class biases in our criminal justice system and the inextricable links between lack of educational opportunity, mental health challenges, and mass incarceration.

Most studies show that the number of people released from prison who wind up returning within three years typically hovers around 40%. This tends to be a statement more about the scarce opportunities these former offenders find on the outside than their predilection for crime. [68]

The data on recidivism make a powerful and compelling case for radical reformation of mass incarceration policies and the dismantling of the constitutive components of the Prison Industrial Complex. Reform versus revolution is a longstanding debate among progressive grassroots activists. Whether to reform or abolish the policies of mass incarceration and the Prison Industrial Complex has been discussed for decades. A powerful case can be made for the wholesale abolition of the PIC—some of the arguments are laid out in this volume. But abolishing incarceration itself is a much more complex issue, given the conventional assumption that some form of prison system is required in modern society.

Abolish All Prisons

Longtime activist and scholar Angela Davis is one of the leaders of the prison abolition movement in the United States. In her book *Are Prisons Obsolete?*, she argues that prisons

> *relieve us of the responsibility of seriously engaging with the problems of our society, especially those produced by racism and, increasingly, global capitalism.*[69]

Professor Davis, who has actively fought the PIC since her own incarceration as a political prisoner in the early 1970s, personally understands the racialized history of the criminal justice system and the sociopolitical consequences of not working toward the abolition of the PIC. The obvious model for the prison abolition movement is the movement to abolish slavery itself. Nineteenth-century abolitionists believed in the basic humanity of enslaved Africans and understood the diminishing effects on the humanity of slave "owners" who worked systemically  to dehumanize their "property." The antislavery movement at its peak was a coalition of Quakers, white Northerners, free Blacks, American Indians, and the enslaved who worked together by nonviolent and violent means to bring about the destruction of the "peculiar institution." So enmeshed was human bondage with the Southern economy that many at the time believed that abolition was impossible—but of course it wasn't.

A number of contemporary scholars, including Michelle Alexander, Douglas Blackmon, and others mentioned in this book, have brilliantly demonstrated the interconnectedness of the policies of mass incarceration, the partnerships in the Prison Industrial

Complex, and the legacy of institutional transatlantic slavery. All have been inextricably linked through a complex history in the United States—a nation that built a global capitalist economic system literally on the backs of enslaved Africans, whose descendants have been systematically overrepresented in a prison system that has expanded tremendously in just the last half-century.

So it seems fitting that a new abolition movement is underway, calling for a complete end to the Prison Industrial Complex. The success of this very important movement depends on our capacity to understand the deep histories that inform the construction of the PIC and the deleterious consequences of our failure to dismantle it as soon as possible.

That said, real reform can be a path to abolition, too. In the absence of a collective political will to rethink the role of prisons in our society and to dismantle the components of the Prison industrial Complex, real reform may be a productive option for undoing some of the damage. According to Michael Jacobson, the author of *Downsizing Prisons* (2006), one of the ironies about real reformation of the PIC is that both privatization and recidivism offer real opportunities to begin shrinking the complex. States that contract with private prisons can cancel, refuse to renew, or resist signing future contracts with private prison corporations like Corrections Corporation of American. They can make it policy not to engage private entities to replace the protections that the criminal justice

system is supposed to provide. By eliminating private contracts with corporations that build, own, and manage prisons, a state can also save money. In 2002, Mississippi closed a CCA prison and realized an almost immediate savings of $4 million.[70]

Directly addressing the challenges of high recidivism offers another opportunity for real reform. Policies rewritten to diminish recidivism rates would eliminate the "technical violation" regulations that make the PIC cyclical for so many paroled inmates. What's called for here is a complete rethinking and overhaul of the parole system. Parole should be administered in reasonable, productive ways based on the tenets of reform and redemption from the early days of the penitentiary. So long as the parole system functions like other aggressive components of the criminal justice system (racial profiling, stop and frisk tactics, no-knock warrants, mandatory minimums, and the like), then it will continue to be a tool of recidivism rather than a process through which prisoners reenter society.

Revising Sentencing

Sentencing reform is critical to any real reformation of the PIC. Advocates and activists must continue to push legislators toward more and more revision of sentencing policy. The goal here is to reform sentencing in a way that funnels nonviolent, lower-level offenders into prison alternatives—giving serious consideration to correctional facilities focused on rehabilitation and community-based practices. Real reform efforts must be organic, emerging in local contexts in ways that address local issues and local concerns. This is especially important for sentencing reform and the challenges of reentry, which are particular to specific communities.

120

Reasonable sentencing should be another important feature of the prison reform effort. Mandatory minimums should be abolished, as they create overly aggressive, overly empowered prosecutors. They give the prosecution too much leverage in the criminal justice system and, in too many ways, eliminate the power of judges to make smarter judicial decisions. Lastly, sentencing disparities that are either inherently or consequently biased by race, class, or gender must be eradicated.

Certain Polices Must Go

Long before criminal court proceedings, the tentacles of the Prison Industrial Complex reach deep into poor communities of color through government policies like the War on Drugs and a wide range of aggressive tactics by local law enforcement. Real reform requires an end to racial profiling, the "broken windows" strategy, stop and frisk tactics, and greater diversity within the ranks of police themselves. Militarizing local law enforcement with combat weapons and the equipment of war will also have to be curtailed if the PIC is ever to be reformed. Policing cannot *look* like warfare if it is to achieve its purpose—to protect and serve—in actuality or in perception.

Indeed there are a great many other considerations for reforming the Prison Industrial Complex, some of them not readily apparent given the overwhelming quantity of data on the prison system itself. Clearly, however, some of the broader societal remedies include a radical reinvestment in public education; ending homelessness and developing more comprehensive affordable housing policies; and decriminalizing certain controlled substances. Given what we know about the War on Drugs, any real reform of the PIC must include the END of the drug war. The War on Drugs is a war on poor people of color, and it has been an abject failure.

Most scholars, reformers, abolitionists, and activists engaged in the struggle to change America's prison addiction also understand that for, all of the possibilities that policy changes represent, real reform must begin with a change in the nation's perception of criminal justice and incarceration. Unless and until the citizenry is ready to wean itself from the abiding sense that punishment is the central purpose of incarceration, the United States will not be able to alter its status as the world's leading incarcerator.

Finally we have to be prepared to *humanize* criminals, and not just the nonviolent ones. Given the scope of the Prison Industrial Complex—its size (2.2 million inmates), its complexity, and the vast economic investments and profits in the system—only a radical revision of how we view crime, criminals, and criminality can move the needle in the right direction. As antidrug advocates often maintain, a harm-reduction approach to drug abuse—or in this case, mass incarceration—is more likely to yield constructive results.

Epilogue

From *The New Jim Crow* to *Jimmy's Back* to *The Last Jimmy*

After leaving central Pennsylvania in 2011, my interest in serving causes that seek to dismantle the PIC never waned. My sense is still that educators have a vital role to play in teaching about the U.S. prison system and in exposing the PIC's complicated presence in our nation's history and its dominance in contemporary society.

The publication of Michelle Alexander's *The New Jim Crow* (2010) and Douglas Blackmon's *Slavery by Any Other Name* (2012) have provided valuable pedagogical tools for educators and policymakers across the spectrum. Reading Alexander's *The New Jim Crow*, and moderating a discussion among public school students after a screening of Blackmon's "Slavery by Another Name" documentary film, I was convinced that the intricacies of the Prison Industrial Complex and its long history could be taught in undergraduate classrooms.

So I designed a course, called "Black Prison Narratives," that attempted to situate the incredible legacy of Black revolutionaries imprisoned prior to the emergence of the PIC within a critical discourse on the history of prisons.[71] I taught the course during the fall semester of 2013, and students told me they were inspired. They, in turn, re-inspired me for the work that must continue if we are ever to be successful in attaining equal treatment under the law for all people in this country. Raising awareness about the structural aspects of the PIC has become an essential aspect of the movements to reform or revolutionize it. In teaching powerful prison narratives by the Rev. Martin Luther King, Jr., Assata Shakur, George Jackson, Angela Davis, and others, critical continuities in the long history of racism and the history of the Prison Industrial Complex became clearer in my mind and the minds of my students.

Later that fall, Karl "Dice Raw" Jenkins, a Philadelphia-based rapper affiliated with The Roots, released a solo album titled *Jimmy's Back*. For me, a fan of Hip Hop music as well as a scholar and critic of the culture, *Jimmy's Back* is an important reminder that Hip Hop artists can sometimes make powerful contributions to the national discourse. Dice Raw's *Jimmy's Back,* inspired by Michelle Alexander's *The New Jim Crow,* is just such a work. For Dice Raw, Alexander's work was a revelation. He had grown up in Philadelphia and witnessed firsthand the kind of aggressive policing associated with the War on Drugs and mass incarceration. But *The New Jim Crow* unveiled for

Jenkins the systematic nature of these policies and placed them in an historical context that he had not previously associated with the critical social outcomes that he saw and reflected upon in his music. So he decided to write and produce an entire recording project inspired by Alexander's incisive work.

The result of his inspiration, *Jimmy's Back*, is a dark reflective portrait of young men besieged by and within the Prison Industrial Complex. Released in late 2013 with little promotion or fanfare, *Jimmy's Back* is a concept album with songs/lyrics that pick up on core themes and insights from Alexander's text. More importantly, *Jimmy's Back* serves as an actual platform for the group of people whom Alexander defines as the "American undercaste"— those who make it out of the PIC but continue to be dogged by the slate of policies that keep ex-convicts out of work, out of public housing, and in many cases back in prison. The album features several artists on various songs, all of them former prisoners locked up as a result of the War on Drugs. Their stories shed piercing rays of light on the lack of economic

opportunity, limited choices, and bad decisions that have contributed to the extraordinary incarceration rates in cities like Philadelphia during the 21st century.

In one particularly poignant song, "Looking Glass," Dice Raw and company explore the existential pain of growing up in a community warped by underground drug economies. The looking glass of the title is both a mirror into the mind state of someone who feels that incarceration is inevitable and the window through which the incarcerated must look in order to communicate with family and friends who visit from outside the system.

"Looking Glass" (from the *Jimmy's Back* album by Dice Raw)

[Refrain]

What do you see through the looking glass
Fallin' when you're looking back
Can't escape walking down this path
Can't live living in the past

[Verse 1]

I see you, I wouldn't want to be you
But it's too late my true face becoming what I already became
And that's my true state, can hurt like a toothache
Looking at ones' true state be exactly what you hate
Trying to find a new slate, think a new mind state
Every kid I grew up with is dead or locked behind gates
I guess it's just a matter of time and I should just wait
Really it's no choice it's just words with no voice
Maybe action the only way to attack it
I'm talking life, trying to be just a little less ratchet
Fuck it nah, I don't like it
I ain't a psychic just by writing this shit yo I don't feel anymore
      righteous
I'm religionless just a nigga on some nigga shit
Truthfully looking in my eyes, I don't give a shit
Not the one to be fucking with

Playing with or kidding with
Cause shit can get real goofy
Fuck all that silly shit

[Refrain]

[Verse 2]

Clothes dirty, gotta hand wash
I'm tired of eatin soups
Going to rack, gotta walk in groups
Seeing my kids but can't touch them
Thinking about time feeling like nothing
Plus I'm fighting you trying to take mine
For me to adjust it's going to take time
Some friends forgot about me, they don't make time
Shit feel like I gotta do a straight dime
Nah, this ain't no place for humans
But I'm strong they ain't think I can make it
But they assuming, gotta read books keep my head straight
Tired of feeling like deadweight
Walk in a child fighting the staircase
I still smile deal with it
Looking through the glass while my fam visit
Some people got forever and a day
Gotta handle what come to you
You can't look the other way, nah

No sign of weakness I would never show it
And if I am nervous they will never know it
Yeah cause I'm a soldier through it all
Fight the pain fact remain I couldn't walk before I crawl

[Verse 3]

Time is measured by movement so I'm tryin to beat the
millennium clock
But I keep going to jail and it feels like my life clock stops
Suspended in time behind bars be fucking with my mind
I'm from the streets so I'm racing passing batons
Hundred yard dashin with a brick, to the finish line
But I got lapped again now I'm trapped again
On that upstate bus I'm going back again
It's like I'm dead to the world nobody writes me
Or come to see me, it's like nobody likes me
All I got is niggas in jail trying to fight me
And the feds building a case trying to indict me

[Lyrics reproduced by permission of the artist.]

The musical style of "Looking Glass" recalls the lamenting tones of a dirge. In effect, the song chronicles the narrator's mourning over personal experience with the Prison Industrial Complex. For the writers and musicians, it is a reflective statement that seeks to capture the pain and frustration of living in a world plagued by systemic forces just beyond critical comprehension of the impact that those forces have on the lives of the vulnerable. The narrators of "Looking Glass" expect empathy more than sympathy, but they also demand that we as a society take a long hard look in the mirror to better understand the reflecting and refracting human consequences of the Prison Industrial Complex.

On listening to *Jimmy's Back,* I was moved to connect with the artists who produced this remarkable recording, inspired as it was by one of the most influential pieces of scholarship on mass incarceration in America. Writer Phillip Brown and theater director Ozzie Jones were equally captivated by Dice Raw's work and developed a Hip Hop musical version of the album that premiered in October 2014. The stage version, titled *The Last Jimmy*, centers on the narrative of a young Black man—the last on the planet not to be incarcerated—and chronicles his experience in a criminal justice system with omnipotent power over his life.

Both the writer and the director of the show were aware of my work on Hip Hop culture and my community service in the Prison Industrial Complex. So they asked me to join the production as the moderator for "talk-back" sessions following nightly performances in Philadelphia and several productions in Los Angeles. Like the album, *The Last Jimmy* channeled Dice Raw's sense of urgency about all the issues surrounding mass incarceration and the Prison Industrial Complex in our contemporary moment. Dialogue with community members from across the nation revealed the fact that, for too many, the policy of mass incarceration has had direct and deleterious effects on their lives and on their neighborhoods.

During one interlude on the album and at a pivotal moment in the play, Wadud Ahmad—a former prosecutor in the Philadelphia District Attorney's Office and an accomplished spoken word poet—points out that "fishing in Black ponds" means that you will catch only "Black fish." This simple statement aptly summarizes the racial disparity endemic to the policy of mass incarceration in America and the overrepresentation of people of color in the Prison Industrial Complex.

Scholarly books, Hip Hop albums, community plays, and even performances at musical award shows all can be enlisted in the ongoing effort to dismantle the Prison Industrial Complex. The problems of the PIC are herculean. The historical roots, complex entanglements, and entrenched power of the social and economic systems that comprise the complex today require an "all hands on deck" mentality to work through the processes of real change. All that that said, the ultimate changes must come in the form of policy initiatives by federal, state, and local governments. Ending the War on Drugs, rethinking the dehumanization of criminals, outlawing private prisons, and rooting out racial bias from the criminal justice system and law enforcement are but a few of the policy shifts necessary to bring an end to the Prison Industrial Complex.

Syllabus: Black Prison Narratives

Professor James B. Peterson

Course Description

This course situates Black prison narratives within the context of the literatures of Social Justice—those novels, poems, lyrics, films, and other texts that directly engage social justice issues. Social Justice can generally be defined as the balance between society's collective accountability with respect to humanity, fairness and equity and the individual's responsibility to be informed about and contribute to these efforts. In this course, confinement, incarceration and later, the emergence of the Prison Industrial Complex and its unchecked interventions into the lives of families and communities of color will all serve as subject matter for a range of literary approaches. Course texts includes Middle Passage narratives, excerpts from Foucault's *Discipline and Punish*, MLK's "Letter from a Birmingham Jail," the PBS documentary *Slavery by Another Name*, Michelle Alexander's *The New Jim Crow,* and other texts, films, and resources that reflect the experience of being black and incarcerated in United States.

Course Objectives

There are several objectives in this course: (1) To survey the history of America's "Penal Democracy," especially it's late-20th Century transition into privatizing the prison system and the emergence of what is often referred to as the Prison Industrial Complex; (2) To come to terms with, interpret, and critique the compelling literature written from within the walls of American prisons; and (3) to explore, research, and write about the social justice concerns at stake for the subjects of the American prison system, as well as their families and communities.

Course Format

This course is an intermediate-level seminar. Students are expected to come to class prepared to discuss the readings or texts assigned for that day. We will regularly spend class time screening films relevant to our subject matter. There will be multiple response papers to films or other texts and some unannounced quizzes. There will be certain on-campus events that we will be required to attend.

Participation and Reading for class is essential. Our classroom discussions will be built around assigned texts, and each student is expected to contribute to these discussions on a regular basis. A significant percentage of your final grade will be based on your overall contribution to in-class discussions. A Facebook page has been created for this course. Please login to Facebook and like the page immediately. This page will serve as a forum for class discourse as well as a resource for more information and texts about the course subject matter. Each Wednesday after class (and before the following Monday—i.e., next class) students are required to post and/or respond to discussion threads on the Black Prison Narratives Facebook page. Posts need not be longer than 50-100 words but everyone is required to post on the page weekly. Students will take turns establishing a question or topic for the threaded discussion.

There will be up to five short answer **Quizzes** given over the course of the term. Each quiz, (worth 10-20 points) will pose questions on the readings for that week and previous in-class discussions. These quizzes will be unannounced.

There will also be an in-class **Examination** that will occur late in the term. This exam will consist of 20 short answer questions, identifications, and/or definitions that you will be required to answer (in detail and on your own) in approximately one class period (i.e. 75 minutes).

There will be a **Response Paper** due one week after the screening of each film. These responses should be 2-4 pages in length (typed, double-spaced, 12-point font) and they require you to reflect upon the most compelling scene, image, concept, or insight that the film impressed upon you.

For the **Final Research Paper** (12-15 pp) students will write a research paper that explores a social justice issue related to race and/or gender and the Prison Industrial Complex. The paper should have a minimum of 10 cited sources. Secondary sources should be academic journal articles or scholarly books on incarceration/confinement and related theories, philosophies, etc. Use MLA format for these papers.

Course Requirements

Class Participation	10%
Social Media Posts	10%
Quizzes	10%
Midterm	30%
Response Papers	20%
Final Research Paper	20%
Total	100%

Course Texts

Pascoe G. Hill	*Fifty Days on board a Slave Vessel* [excerpt]
Michel Foucault	*Discipline & Punish* [excerpt]
Martin L. King	"Letter from a Birmingham Jail"
Assata Shakur	*Assata: An Autobiography*
George Jackson	*Soledad Brother: The Prison Letters of George Jackson*
Angela Davis	*The Meaning of Freedom and Other Difficult Dialogues Abolition Democracy: Beyond Empire, Prisons and Torture*
Michelle Alexander	*The New Jim Crow*
Paul Butler	*Let's Get Free: A Hip Hop Theory of Justice*
Allen Hornblum	*Sentenced to Science: One Black Man's Story of Imprisonment in America*
Percey Carey	*Sentences: The Life of MF Grimm*

Course Films

Slavery by Another Name
The Central Park Five
The House I Live In
The Middle of Nowhere.

Class/Topic Schedule (subject to change)

Introduction, resources, expectations, etc.
Slave Vessel excerpt, "Prison Horrors" and D&P excerpt
"Letter from a Birmingham Jail" and "Democracy & Captivity"
Assata (pp 1- 98)
Assata (pp. 99-274)

In-class (*Slavery by Another Name*) begin *Soledad Brother*
Soledad Brother (pp 1-200)
Soledad Brother (pp 200 – 339)
(Sentencing Project.com) 3 min pres. [Response Paper Due]
Abolition Democracy
In-class listening to Angela Davis
The Meaning of Freedom (pp. 1- 86)
The Meaning of Freedom (pp. 87-201)
"Cruel but Not Unusual" & "An Interview with Shake Sankofa"
The New Jim Crow
The New Jim Crow (begin screening *The Central Park Five)*
In-class screening *The Central Park Five*
Flashback: research and discuss "The Scottsboro Boys"
Exam Review [Response Paper Due]
EXAM (20-25 Short Answer Questions)
In-Class screening, *The House I Live In;* begin *Let's Get Free*
Let's Get Free (pp. 1-121)
Let's Get Free (pp. 122-185)
Sentenced to Science (pp. 1 – 99)
Sentenced to Science (pp. 100 – 200)
Sentences: The Life of MF Grimm
Online: Best of Our Class Discussions on Facebook
Final Response Paper Due
Discussion of Topics – Final Research Paper

Notes

[1] Thompson, Heather Ann. "Why Mass Incarceration Matters: Rethinking Crisis, Decline and Transformation in Postwar American History," *Journal of American History.* (December, 2010).

[2] Muhammad, Khalil Gibran. *The Condemnation of Blackness: Race, Crime and the Making of Modern Urban America.* Cambridge: Harvard University Press, 2010.

[3] Steven R. Donziger, ed. *The Real War on Crime: The Report of the National Criminal Justice Commission.* New York: HarperCollins Books, 1996 p. 87.

[4] Sabrina Jones and Marc Mauer. *Race to Incarcerate: A Graphic Retelling.* New York: The New Press, 2013 pp 5-6.

[5] Norval Morris and David Rothman, eds. *The Oxford History of the Prison: The Practice of Punishment in Western Society.* New York: Oxford University Press, 1998, pp. 105-6.

[6] Norval Morris and David Rothman, eds. *The Oxford History of the Prison: The Practice of Punishment in Western Society.* New York: Oxford University Press, 1998, pp. 106.

[7] Ibid., 105.

[8] Ibid., 107.

[9] Ibid.

[10] Ibid., 106

[11] This early iteration of solitary confinement is not to be confused with the tortuous form of solitary confinement discussed in Chapter Five.

[12] Michel Foucault. *Discipline and Punish: The Birth of the Prison.* New York: Vintage Books, 1995, p. 239.

[13] Norval Morris and David Rothman, eds. *The Oxford History of the Prison: The Practice of Punishment in Western Society*. New York: Oxford University Press, 1998, p. 105.

[14] Christie, Nils. *Crime Control as Industry: Towards Gulags, Western Style*. London: Routledge, 1993.

[15] Kidd, David. "The Sounds of Silence in Prison." Governing: The State and Localities. http://www.governing.com/topics/public-justice-safety/gov-prison-sounds-of-silence.html Last Accessed 09/14/2015.

[16] Davis, Angela. *Are Prisons Obsolete?* New York: Seven Stories Press, 2003, p. 84-85.

[17] Davis, Mike. "Hell Factories in the Field." *The Nation*. February 20, 1995.

[18] Glassner, Barry. *The Culture of Fear: Why Americans are Afraid of the Wrong Things*. New York: Basic Books, 1999.

[19] Steven R. Donziger, ed. *The Real War on Crime: The Report of the National Criminal Justice Commission*. New York: HarperCollins Books, 1996.

[20] Steven R. Donziger, ed. *The Real War on Crime: The Report of the National Criminal Justice Commission*. New York: HarperCollins Books, 1996 p. 85.

[21] Wehr, Kevin and Elyshia Aseltine. *Beyond the Prison Industrial Complex: Crime and Incarceration in the 21st Century*. New York: Routledge, 2013 p. 1.

[22] Ibid. p. 1.

[23] Data and percentages detailed in reports from the US Department of Education's National Center for Education Statistics, 2010-2011.

[24] Shipp, Robbin and Nick Chiles. *Justice While Black: Helping African American Families Navigate and Survive the Criminal Justice System*. Chicago: Bolden/Agate, 2014 p. 121.

[25] Childs, Dennis. *Slaves of the State: Black Incarceration from the Chain Gang to the Penitentiary.* Minneapolis: University of Minnesota Press, 2015: p. 21.

[26] Glave, E.J. *In Savage Africa.* 1892: p. 190.

[27] Blackmon, Douglas. *Slavery by Another Name.*

[28] Leflouria, Talitha L. *Chained in Silence: Black Women and Convict Labor in the New South.* Chapel Hill: University of North Carolina Press, 2015: p 5.

[29] Jones, Sabrina, and Marc Mauer. *Race to Incarcerate: A Graphic Retelling.* New York: 2013: p. 19.

[30] Martinson, Robert. "What works? - questions and answers about prison reform." *National Affairs.* Issue No. 34, Spring 1974: p. 49.

[31] Ibid.

[32] "A Brief History of the Drug War." http://www.drugpolicy.org/new-solutions-drug-policy/brief-history-drug-war. Last Accessed December 10, 2015.

[33] https://web.stanford.edu/class/e297c/poverty_prejudice/paradox/htele.html Last Accessed December 10 2015.

[34] Kilgore, James. *Understanding Mass Incarceration: A People's Guide to the Key Civil Rights Struggle of Our Time.* New York: The New Press, 2015: 59.

[35] https://web.stanford.edu/class/e297c/poverty_prejudice/paradox/htele.html Last Accessed December 10 2015.

[36] http://www.drugpolicy.org/new-solutions-drug-policy/brief-history-drug-war Last Accessed December 30, 2015.

[37] Kilgore, James. *Understanding Mass Incarceration: A People's Guide to the Key Civil Rights Struggle of Our Time.* New York: The New Press, 2015: 60.

[38]http://www.drugpolicy.org/new-solutions-drug-policy/brief-history-drug-war Last Accessed December 30, 2015.

[39]http://www.drugpolicy.org/new-solutions-drug-policy/brief-history-drug-war Last Accessed December 21, 2015.

[40] Kilgore, James. *Understanding Mass Incarceration: A People's Guide to the Key Civil Rights Struggle of Our Time.* New York: The New Press, 2015: 65.

[41] NAFTA, or the North American Free Trade Agreement, went into effect on January 1, 1994; CAFTA, the Central America Free Trade Agreement, went into effect on March 1, 2006; and TPP is the proposed Trans-Pacific Partnership.

[42] Goldberg, Eve and Linda Evans. *The Prison Industrial Complex and the Global Economy.* Oakland, CA: Agit Press 2009: 9.

[43] As discussed a bit more in Chapter One.

[44] Goldberg, Eve and Linda Evans. *The Prison Industrial Complex and the Global Economy.* Oakland, CA: Agit Press 2009: 8.

[45] Kilgore, James. *Understanding Mass Incarceration: A People's Guide to the Key Civil Rights Struggle of Our Time.* New York: The New Press, 2015: 183.

[46] Ibid.

[47]https://www.popularresistance.org/identifying-businesses-that-profit-from-prison-labor/ Last Accessed January 10, 2016.

[48] Kilgore, James. *Understanding Mass Incarceration: A People's Guide to the Key Civil Rights Struggle of Our Time.* New York: The New Press, 2015: 168.

[49] Cohen, Michael. "How for-profit prisons have become the biggest lobby no one is talking about." https://www.washingtonpost.com/posteverything/wp/2015/04/28/how-for-profit-prisons-have-become-the-biggest-lobby-no-one-is-talking-about/ Last accessed December 28, 2015.

50 Ibid., 169.

51 AFSC. http://afsc.org/resource/arizona-prison-report
Last Accessed December 8 2015.

52 Owen, Jonathan. "Selfharm, drug-taking and sexual abuse more
common in privately run prisons, new figures show." Published
April 4 2015. http://www.independent.co.uk/news/uk/crime/
self-harm-drug-taking-and-sexual-abuse-more-common-in-
privately-run-prisons-new-figures-show-10156397.html   Last
Accessed December 8th 2015.

53 Brickner, Michael and Shakyra Diaz. "Prisons for Profit:
Incarceration for Sale." *Human Rights Magazine* (ACLU) Summer
2011, Vol. 38 No. 3. http://www.americanbar.org/publications/
human_rights_magazine_home/human_rights_vol38_2011/
human_rights_summer11/prisons_for_profit_incarceration_for_
sale.html Last Accessed December 10, 2015.

54 Lotke, Eric. "The Real Problem with Private Prisons." http://
www.huffingtonpost.com/eric-lotke/the-real-problem-with-
pri_b_8279488.html Last accessed April 11, 2016.

55 DiIullio, John K., William Bennett, and John P. Walters, *Body Count:
Moral Poverty and How to Win America's War on Crime and
Drugs.* New York: Simon & Schuster, 1996.

56 Johnson, Corey G. and Ken Armstrong. "This Boy's Life." https://
www.themarshallproject.org/2016/01/04/this-boy-s-life#.
tgeuG78hJ. Last Accessed August 21, 2016.

57 Wessler, Seth F. "This Man Will Almost Certainly Die." http://www.
thenation.com/article/privatized-immigrant-prison-deaths/
Last Accessed March 4, 2016.

58 http://www.afsc.org/resource/solitary-confinement-facts

59 http://www.afsc.org/resource/solitary-confinement-facts

60 Kilgore, James. *Understanding Mass Incarceration: A People's Guide
to the Key Civil Rights Struggle of Our Time.* New York: The New
Press, 2015: 91.

[61] Steven R. Donziger, ed. *The Real War on Crime: The Report of the National Criminal Justice Commission.* New York: HarperCollins Books, 1996: 74-75.

[62] Ibid.

[63] Jacobson, Michael. *Downsizing Prisons: How to Reduce Crime and End Mass Incarceration.* New York: New York University Press, 2005: 24.

[64] Ibid.

[65] "The Second Chance Act." https://csgjusticecenter.org/nrrc/projects/second-chance-act/

[66] Kilgore, James. *Understanding Mass Incarceration: A People's Guide to the Key Civil Rights Struggle of Our Time.* New York: The New Press, 2015: 94.

[67] Kilgore, James. *Understanding Mass Incarceration: A People's Guide to the Key Civil Rights Struggle of Our Time.* New York: The New Press, 2015: 91

[68] Shipp, Robbin and Nick Chiles. *Justice While Black: Helping African-American Families Navigate and Survive the Criminal Justice System.* Chicago: Bolden/Agate, 2014: 152.

[69] Davis, Angela. *Are Prisons Obsolete?*

[70] Jacobson, Michael. *Downsizing Prisons: How to Reduce Crime and End Mass Incarceration.* New York: New York University Press, 2005: 176.

[71] The syllabus for this course is included in an appendix to this volume.

Further Reading

Alexander, Michelle. *The New Jim Crow: Mass Incarceration in the Time of Colorblindness.* New York: New Press, 2010.

Bernstein, Nell. *Burning Down the House: The End of Juvenile Prison.* New York: New Press, 2014.

Blackmon, Douglas. *Slavery by Another Name: The Re-Enslavement of Black Americans from the Civil War to World War II.* New York: Anchor Books, 2009.

Butler, Paul. *Let's Get Free: A Hip-Hop Theory of Justice.* New York: New Press, 2009.

Childs, Dennis. *Slaves of the State: Black Incarceration from the Chain Gang to the Penitentiary.* Minneapolis: University of Minnesota Press, 2015.

Christie, Nils. *Crime Control as Industry: Towards Gulags, Western Style.* New York: Routledge, 1993.

Coates, Ta-nehisi. "The Black Family in the Age of Mass Incarceration." *The Atlantic,* October 2015.

Davis, Angela. *Are Prisons Obsolete?* New York: Seven Stories, 2003.

Foucault, Michel. *Discipline and Punish: The Birth of the Prison.* New York: Vintage, 1995.

Fortner, Michael Javen. *Black Silent Majority: The Rockefeller Drug Laws and the Politics of Punishment.* Cambridge, MA: Harvard University Press, 2015.

Gibran Muhammad, Khalil. *The Condemnation of Blackness: Race, Crime, and the Making of Modern Urban America.* Cambridge, MA: Harvard University Press, 2010.

Gross, Kali N. *Colored Amazons: Crime, Violence, and Black Women in the City of Brotherly Love, 1880-1910.* Durham, NC: Duke University Press, 2006.

Jacobson, Michael. *Downsizing Prisons: How to Reduce Crime and End Mass Incarceration.* New York: New York University Press, 2005.

James, Joy, ed. *The New Abolitionists: (Neo) Slave Narratives and Contemporary Prison Writings.* Albany: State University of New York Press, 2005.

Jones, Sabrina, and Marc Mauer. *Race to Incarcerate: A Graphic Retelling.* New York: New Press, 2013.

Kilgore, James. *Understanding Mass Incarceration: A People's Guide to the Key Civil Rights Struggle of Our Time.* New York: New Press, 2015.

LeFlouria, Talitha. *Chained in Silence: Black Women and Convict Labor in the New South.* Chapel Hill: University of North Carolina

Press, 2015.

Mauer, Mark, and Meda Chesney, Lind, eds. *Invisible Punishment: The Collateral Consequences of Mass Imprisonment.* New York: New Press, 2002.

Morris, Norval, and David Rothman, eds. *The Oxford History of the Prison: The Practice of Punishment in Western Society.* New York: Oxford University Press, 1998.

Schenwar, Maya. *Locked Down, Locked Out: Why Prison Doesn't Work and How We Can Do Better.* San Francisco: Berrett-Koehler, 2014.

Shipp, Robbin. *Justice While Black: Helping African-American Families Navigate and Survive the Criminal Justice System.* Chicago: Bolden/Agate, 2014.

Taylor, Caitlin J., and Kathleen Auerhahn. "Community Justice and Public Safety: Assessing Criminal Justice Policy through the Lens of the Social Contract." *Criminology & Criminal Justice,* 15(3): 300-320, 2015.

Thompson, Heather Ann. "Why Mass Incarceration Matters: Rethinking Crisis, Decline and Transformation in Postwar American History," *Journal of American History.* (December, 2010).

Wehr, Kevin, and Elyshia Aseltine. *Beyond the Prison Industrial Complex: Crime and Incarceration in the 21st Century.* New York: Routledge, 2013.

FREEDOM

TO THE PEOPLE!

About the Author

James Braxton Peterson is Director of Africana Studies and Associate Professor of English at Lehigh University. He has written and lectured extensively on the intersection of race, politics, and popular culture in America, with a focus on the criminal justice system, prisons, and hip-hop. He is a frequent media commentator, appearing on MSNBC, CNN, Al-Jazeera, HLN, Fox News, and other networks, and regular blogger for the  Huffington Post. He hosts a radio show called "The Remix" on WHYY, the NPR radio affiliate in Philadelphia, and his first book was *The Hip Hop Underground and African American Culture* (Palgrave Macmillan, 2014).

About the Illustrators

John Jennings is a Professor of Media and Cultural Studies at the University of California at Riverside. His work centers around intersectional narratives regarding identity politics and popular media. Jennings is co-editor of the Eisner Award winning collection The Blacker the Ink: Constructions of Black Identity in Comics and Sequential Art and co-founder/organizer of The Schomburg Center's Black Comic Book Festival in Harlem. He is co-founder and organizer of the  MLK NorCal's Black Comix Arts Festival in San Francisco and also SOL-CON: The Brown and Black Comix Expo at the Ohio State University. Jennings is currently a Nasir Jones Hip Hop Studies Fellow with the Hutchins Center at Harvard University. Jennings' current comics projects include the Hiphop adventure comic Kid Code: Channel Zero, the supernatural crime noir story Blue Hand Mojo, and the upcoming graphic novel adaptation of Octavia Butler's classic dark fantasy novel Kindred.

Stacey Robinson is an Assistant Professor of Graphic Design at the University of Illinois at Urbana-Champaign. He's an Arthur Schomburg fellow who completed his Masters of Fine Art at the University at Buffalo. Stacey is originally from Albany NY and graduated from Fayetteville State University with a Bachelor of Arts. His art speculates futures where Black people are free from colonial influences to explore the possibilities of what that means. His recent exhibition 'Binary ConScience' explores ideas of W. E. B. Du Bois's "double consciousness" as a Black cultural adaptation and a means of colonial survival. He along with John Jennings is part of the collaborative duo 'Black Kirby' that explores Afro Speculative existence via the aesthetic of Jack Kirby. He recently art directed 'Unveiling Visions: the Alchemy of the Black Imagination' for the Schomburg Center for Research in Black Culture in Harlem, NY. He was a part of the exhibition Invisible Ink: Black Independent Comix, at University of Tennessee at Beyond the Frame: African American Comic Book Artists, Presentation at the Flint Institute of Arts. Stacey's collected works reside: Modern Graphics in Berlin, Bucknell University and the Schomburg Center for Research in Black Culture.

Black Kirby is the collaborative imaginings of John Jennings and Stacey Robinson. As a collective entity, Black Kirby explores Afro-speculative futures by examining the Black traumatic past and present via the aesthetic of modern comic's creator Jack Kirby. Black Kirby works can found in the pages of 'Kid Code: Channel Zero' from Rosarium Publishing and the catalogue titled 'Black Kirby Presents: In Search of...The Motherboxx Connection, an art exhibition' from Cedar Grove Publishing.

BLACK KIRBY Gallery